High Seas and Yankee Gunboats

STUDIES IN MARITIME HISTORY

WILLIAM N. STILL, JR., SERIES EDITOR

RECENT TITLES

Iron Afloat: The Story of the Confederate Armorclads
William N. Still, Jr.

To California by Sea: A Maritime History of the Gold Rush
James P. Delgado

Lifeline of the Confederacy: Blockade Running during the Civil War
Stephen R. Wise

The Lure of Neptune: German-Soviet Naval Collaboration and Ambitions
Tobias R. Philbin III

High Seas Confederate: The Life and Times of John Newland Maffitt
Royce Shingleton

The Defeat of the German U-Boats: The Battle of the Atlantic
David Syrett

John P. Holland, 1841–1914: Inventor of the Modern Submarine
Richard Knowles Morris

Cockburn and the British Navy in Transition:
Admiral Sir George Cockburn, 1772–1853
Roger Morriss

The Royal Navy in European Waters during the
American Revolutionary War
David Syrett

Sir John Fisher's Naval Revolution
Nicholas A. Lambert

Forty-Niners 'round the Horn
Charles R. Schultz

The Abandoned Ocean
Andrew Gibson and Arthur Donovan

Northern Naval Superiority and the Economics of the American Civil War
David G. Surdam

Ironclads and Big Guns of the Confederacy:
The Journal and Letters of John M. Brooke
Edited by George M. Brooke, Jr.

High Seas and Yankee Gunboats:
A Blockade-Running Adventure from the Diary of James Dickson
Roger S. Durham

High Seas and Yankee Gunboats

A BLOCKADE-RUNNING ADVENTURE FROM THE DIARY OF JAMES DICKSON

Roger S. Durham

University of South Carolina Press

© 2005 University of South Carolina

Published in Columbia, South Carolina,
by the University of South Carolina Press

Manufactured in the United States of America

09 08 07 06 05   5 4 3 2 1

Library of Congress Cataloging-in-Publication Data

Durham, Roger S.
   High seas and Yankee gunboats : a blockade-running adventure from the diary of James
Dickson/
Roger S. Durham.
      p. cm.— (Studies in maritime history)
   Includes bibliographical references and index.
   ISBN 1-57003-572-5 (cloth : alk. paper)
   1. United States—History—Civil War, 1861-1865—Blockades. 2. Dickson, James, b. 1835 or 6.
3. Hernandez, Thomas L. 4. Sailors—Confederate States of America—Diaries. I. Title. II.
Series.
   E600.D87 2005
   973.7'5—dc22

                                                                        2004022123

Dedicated to Mr. William P. Kellam and Mr. Robert M. Willingham Jr.,
without whom this story might never have been told, and to my wife, JoAnn,
who was there at the beginning and all along the way.

CONTENTS

List of Illustrations / ix
Preface / xi
Acknowledgments / xv

Chapter 1
Prelude / 1

Chapter 2
Bound for Nova Scotia / 12

Chapter 3
Bound for Georgia / 37

Chapter 4
Results and Consequences / 85

Chapter 5
Time to Pay the Piper / 114

Chapter 6
Aftermath / 140

Chapter 7
Postlude / 158

Notes / 169
Bibliography / 177
Index / 181

ILLUSTRATIONS

Figures

Thomas L. Hernandez / 10
Little Cranberry Island beach / 24
Cape Split / 29
E. C. Churchill shipyard at Hantsport / 30
Windsor Bridge / 32
Aerial view of modern-day Halifax / 35
Four Mile House / 35
View of Halifax from the Citadel / 38
Aerial view of the Citadel / 40
View of the entrance to Halifax Harbor / 41
View of Halifax from Georges Island / 42
Remains of the causeway near the South End House / 82
Telephoto of the causeway remains / 83
Rev. Charles C. Jones / 92
Montevideo Plantation House / 92
Mrs. Mary Jones / 94
Children of Reverend and Mrs. Jones / 94
Robert Q. Mallard and Mary Sharpe Jones with
Mallard's mother / 95
Charles C. Jones Jr. / 95
Joseph Jones / 96
Alexander A. Semmes / 108
William A. Fleming and his wife / 112
Melon Bluff / 119
Montevideo boat landing / 131
Half Moon Bluff, looking west / 136

Looking downstream from Half Moon Bluff / 137
CSS *Atlanta* / 152
U.S. officers on the deck of the CSS *Atlanta* / 153
Tom Hernandez with the crew of the CSS *Atlanta* / 153
Hernandez plot in Laurel Grove Cemetery / 155
Dickson plot in Laurel Grove Cemetery / 156

Maps

Mount Desert Island / 21
Destination: Halifax / 25
Halifax Harbor / 36
The Georgia Coast / 66
Sapelo Sound / 70
Liberty County / 88

PREFACE

The War between the States was a massive conflict covering thousands of square miles of land and water and composed of a multitude of large and small events. Many of the unsung heroes of that war are lost to us today because they were involved in events of no real significance to the outcome of the conflict. Their bravery did nothing to shape the course of the war or the history of human events, yet each such incident had its impact on those who lived it. This book is about some of these heroes.

The Civil War divided our country along many lines, such as regional, economic and political. The Northern states faced off against the Southern states, and patriots on both sides swore allegiance to their causes. But there were those who swore allegiance to the dollar, and the war presented them an enormous opportunity to make money. This was particularly true after Lincoln established a naval blockade of the Southern ports, which was intended to keep the South from receiving outside assistance and supplies and to keep Southern shipping from carrying out Southern cotton and produce. The blockade was an ambitious undertaking and could not be established overnight. But eventually it was established and became an efficient mechanism for the North toward bringing the war to a successful conclusion.

In the early months of the war, all manner of ships were pressed into service as blockade gunboats and as blockade runners. The blockade was easily penetrated at this time, and as commercial commodities became scarce in the South, many people were encouraged to invest in blockade-running ventures. The profit margins were often enormous, and in many instances a successful run through the blockade could result in a profit sufficient to pay for the vessel that carried the cargo through the blockade. For some ventures companies were organized to conduct trade running the blockade, while others were efforts undertaken by individuals not backed by companies.

This book is the story of two men and their attempt to run the blockade of the Georgia coast in early 1862. The narrative traces the journey of James Dickson and his friend Thomas L. Hernandez, both from Savannah, Georgia. Their story begins in Newark, New Jersey, where Dickson lived. Then they they were smuggled out of Jersey City to Nova Scotia, where they boarded the blockade runner *Standard* for their trip to Georgia. It was no pleasure cruise, and the storms they encountered were so severe that it took them more than five weeks to make their voyage. The narrative is drawn from a diary that James Dickson kept during the voyage to record his thoughts and the events that transpired around him. However, the Dickson diary itself was a puzzling document, coming to an abrupt end in mid-sentence, concluding, without closure, a four-month narrative. Only now have the previously missing pieces of the puzzle revealed the untold portion of Dickson's story and put it into the perspective of its time.

Through Dickson's diary we follow the crew of the brigantine *Standard* as they struggle through north Atlantic storms to bring their cargo to Savannah. The *Standard,* being sail-powered, was at an obvious disadvantage when pitted against steam-powered blockade gunboats. But such was the disdain and contempt these men felt for the efficiency of the blockade that they staked everything on this sail-powered brigantine to carry them to a successful conclusion. In spite of numerous obstacles and crises, in the end, they did bring their cargo through to Savannah.

In the later years of the war, the blockade became more effective, and ships were built specifically to serve as blockade gunboats or blockade runners as all evolved to the most efficient forms in both extremes. However, early in the war, it was anybody's game, and the prizes they played for were often quite valuable. This is the story of a group of men who took the gamble, as told through the eyes of one of its members. While Dickson and his comrades felt that the Yankee blockaders were their biggest threat, in reality, it was Mother Nature and Human Nature that proved to be their biggest obstacles.

But there is more to this story than the obvious historical elements. It is also about how intricate life is and how the actions and decisions of people affect others, even people who do not know one another or who have not lived in the same period. It is about how people interact with other people and, in so doing, weave the intricate fabric of life that we look back on as history. It is about how Fate plays a role in each of our lives, many times without our even knowing it.

The story behind the story, that of how this historical narrative was uncovered and came to be told today, is as curious and ironic as the events of a century earlier. It was a simple twist of fate that led to this story being uncovered; the editor soon found himself propelled on a journey across time and geography. Thus, this book allows us to look into one small facet of that great conflict known as the Civil War, and to gain, through knowledge of the lives of people who lived a hundred years before us, a better understanding of how our lives and actions affect others.

Editorial Statement

To the best of my ability, I have tried to compile a factual, documented, and historically accurate narrative of these events. Some content was reorganized in order to make it more readable, and some spelling and grammatical errors were corrected in order to make their reading a little easier, but this in no way alters or affects the contents or the meaning of the documents in question. In some instances I have inserted missing words or letters, within brackets, to denote the place where they should have been located. Material that has been omitted is noted with an ellipsis. Some documents, such as the Dickson diary, was written without capitalization or punctuation in many instances. In these cases I have inserted the proper capital letters or punctuation as necessary.

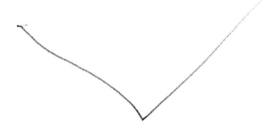

ACKNOWLEDGMENTS

This work has taken many years, and many people and institutions have contributed to it. First and foremost, the following institutions and their personnel are to be acknowledged for their assistance in this work:

Dalhousie University Library—Halifax, Nova Scotia
Emory University Library—Decatur, Georgia
Georgia Department of Natural Resources
Georgia Historical Society—Savannah, Georgia
Mary Willis Library—Washington, Georgia
Midway Museum—Midway, Georgia
Museum of the City of New York—New York, New York
New-York Historical Society—New York, New York
Nova Scotia Communication and Information Center—Halifax, Nova Scotia
Nova Scotia Archives and Records Management—Halifax, Nova Scotia
Tulane University Library—New Orleans, Louisiana
University of Georgia Library—Athens, Georgia

A number of individuals deserve mention as their contributions and assistance was invaluable along the way. The one person who probably planted the seeds for this whole project was Mr. William P. Kellam of the University of Georgia Library, who brought the James Dickson diary to its present home in Athens, Georgia, and laid the foundation for subsequent research.

Mr. Robert M. "Skeet" Willingham Jr. was the individual who insisted that I pay him a visit at the University of Georgia Library and investigate the material in its manuscript collection. It was on my first visit to "Skeet" that I found the Dickson diary. The rest, as they say, is history. Mr. Richard Harwell, also of the University of Georgia

Library, was the individual who encouraged me to pursue my research into the Dickson diary and the story that was there and to get it published.

In Nova Scotia a number of people were instrumental in providing me with necessary assistance to locate the "needle in the haystack" that I was trying to find there. Foremost among these individuals was Mr. Bruce Parsons, who indeed was "just the person" I needed to see and helped me make the most efficient use of the limited time I had there. I think Bruce Parsons has a story of his own to tell, but he is too busy living it to worry about telling it. He and Tom Hernandez are probably kindred spirits. Mr. J. Carnell, of Birch Cove, Nova Scotia, was the person who put it all together for me and pointed me in the right direction just when I needed it. I think I was led to him at just the right time. Mr. Bruce Nunn, the Nova Scotia "know-it-all," was very helpful in providing me with a forum through an interview he conducted with me for his radio program in Halifax. It was through this program that I was lead to Ms. Sharon Ingalls of the Rockingham Historical Society, who had information on the Donaldson and Dickson families of Birch Cove.

Ms. Julie Eden of Philadelphia, Pennsylvania, is another "twist of fate" whose postcard request for a park brochure opened the door to my learning more about Pendleton G. Watmough, since she lived just down the street from where his home once stood. I would also be remiss if I did not acknowledge the reseach her daughter conducted on my behalf in finding the information on Watmough and his family, which she took on as a summer project since she did not have anything else to do at the time.

A special thanks is due Ms. Nancy Pelletier of Lewiston, Maine, who was the custodian of a rare CDV image of Tom Hernandez and graciously made it available to me for inclusion in this book. Now everyone can look into the eyes of Tom Hernandez and ponder the events he witnessed.

Mr. Lynn Holman, of Colonel's Island, Georgia, was instrumental in providing me with nautical support for my expeditions along the coast to seek out the many places where this history happened. He was always ready to take on another adventure at a moment's notice and was a stalwart companion through it all. We stomped through dense woods and across the muddy marshes, were stranded on the beach at Black-beard Island, and fought sand gnats and rattlesnakes; Lynn took it all in stride, with no complaint. He provided the boat, knowledge of the coastal waterways, and accommodations when necessary. I could not have done it without him.

I have always appreciated the support and encouragement of Don, Laura, and Meredith Devendorf of Midway, Georgia. Melon Bluff has been in Laura's family for many years, and through their generosity people can still visit Melon Bluff today and see it much the way that James Dickson and Tom Hernandez did.

A special thanks goes to Dr. Stephen R. Wise, director of the Parris Island Museum, who directed me to the University of South Carolina Press and to Mr. Alexander Moore, my acquisitions editor, who took an interest in this project and guided me through the process to get this story into print after all the years of working with it.

There are many others who have contributed to this effort in many ways. It would be impossible to name them all, but this small book is a tribute to everyone's efforts on my behalf, and to James and Tom as well.

Throughout it all, my wife, JoAnn, was my constant companion. She was there when I found the Dickson diary; suffered silently without a word of complaint as I labored at the typewriter and computer over the years; and accompanied me on many of the expedtions to the Georgia coast and also on the journey to Nova Scotia. Her quiet support was an essential contribution to the fact that this project came together.

High Seas and Yankee Gunboats

·⇒ ONE ⇐·

Prelude

n 1860 regional differences between the North and South over issues such as states rights and slavery reached crisis proportions and threatened to tear the United States apart. Fanatical groups produced much furor over the issues, and cooler heads were lost in the rattling of sabers and the rush of patriots to their causes. There were no simple answers, and it seemed that all the compromises had been tried. The time had come for the country to face problems that could no longer be avoided.

In November 1860 Abraham Lincoln was elected president of the United States as a result of divided Southern political parties. His election was repugnant to the Southerners, and a convention of Southern states was called to discuss a course of action. On 20 December 1860 South Carolina boldly took action on its own by seceding from the union of states. In due time its example was followed by other Southern states, and soon after the Confederacy stood in resistance to "Yankee Rule." The nation stood at a crossroads in its history. The storm of war broke across the land in April 1861 with the bombardment of Fort Sumter in Charleston, South Carolina, where a group of U.S. soldiers had been holding out, refusing to turn over the fort to Confederate authorities. There was no longer any choice as to what road the nation would take, for it was now firmly on the road to war.

In Washington, D.C., President Lincoln tried to pull the Federal government together. He issued a call for volunteers to suppress the rebellion, and volunteers rallied from all across the Northern states, just as their Southern counterparts were doing in a similar response to their own country's need. He also declared his intention to blockade the Southern ports and coastline, and on 13 April, the day Fort Sumter fell, the frigate USS *Sabine* officially initiated Lincoln's blockade by taking up a position off Pensacola, Florida.

Lincoln's idea to establish a blockade was ridiculed by many, even by members of his own cabinet. To enforce a blockade of 3,549 miles of Southern coastline with 189 bays, rivers, and inlets seemed nothing less than an impossibility as the U.S. Navy had only a small number of seaworthy ships on hand at that time. The rest of the fleet was scattered on different service around the world, and it would take time to call it home. Lincoln remained firm in his belief that closing off the Southern ports was essential, and he established the Navy Blockade Board, which was tasked to carry out this mission. The navy immediately launched a program to purchase and build the necessary vessels that would be needed to implement and enforce the blockade. Everything from passenger steamers to ferryboats was purchased, converted, outfitted, and armed for blockading service with the navy.[1]

The Southerners scoffed at Federal efforts to blockade their coast. They were trying to build a navy of their own, but most people felt that the war would be over long before the blockade could have any effect. Through the first months of the war the blockade was at best a token threat as the Southern coastline favored the blockade runners rather than the blockaders. An officer aboard the USS *Iroquois,* stationed off Savannah, wrote in disgust: "We are some 12 miles from the shore; can just see the outlines of land and that is all. . . . The blockade is a perfect farce, I think, for we can see steamers run up and down the coast every day, and we are so far off that we are useless; before we could get underway they could be out of sight."[2] Sailors assigned to the blockading vessels had to keep a sharp eye on the coast to spot any outward-bound craft and also toward the sea to sight any approaching ships. But such an ambitious undertaking as the blockade of the extensive Southern coast could not be expected to succeed overnight. It would have to be instituted in phases.

In August 1861 the first striking force sent out by the U.S. Navy attacked at Hatteras Inlet on the barrier islands of the North Carolina coast. Here the Union forces overpowered the Confederate defenders and took possession of the area. This was the first offensive move taken to strengthen the blockade, but the victory was of little interest to most Northern people, who could not grasp the importance of the naval strategy. Most people on both sides still expected the war to be won by land battles and not naval victories.

In Washington, D.C., the Navy Blockade Board struggled to decide how best to institute and enforce the blockade. To be truly effective, a coaling station, repair facility, and supply depot needed to be established at a strategic point along the southeast coast to support the blockading vessels. To secure and build this depot would be the next major step in strengthening the infant blockade. Once this base had been built, further measures could be taken to escalate the blockade's effectiveness. Charts and maps were studied in great detail to determine where this support facility should be located. Between Fortress Monroe at Hampton Roads, Virginia, and Fort Pickens at Pensacola, Florida, there were no locations in Federal control that could provide the necessary support. Hatteras was only an inlet through sandbars and could not serve as a suitable base of operations.

While discussions took place as to where to establish this support base, a massive expedition of ships, men, and matériel was being assembled to seize the designated area once it had been determined. In September 1861 Secretary of the Navy Gideon Welles finally placed the decision in the hands of the two men who were to lead the expedition—Adm. Samuel F. Du Pont, a fifty-eight-year-old native of New Jersey who had served with the navy since 1815, and Brig. Gen. Thomas W. Sherman, a forty-eight-year-old native of Rhode Island and an 1836 graduate of West Point.[3]

After weeks of discussion and prodding from Washington, these two men agreed that Hilton Head Island, South Carolina, was the perfect location. Port Royal Sound, north of the island, offered a natural deepwater harbor, and the island was located almost directly between Savannah and Charleston. A vital railroad linked these two cities and lay inland within easy striking distance. Also, the climate was suitable for year-round operations against Charleston and Savannah. On 29 October 1861 the decision was made to attack and seize Hilton Head Island.[4]

The ships of the expedition waited for weeks off Hampton Roads, Virginia, for the signal to begin the grand operation. It was an impressive sight, for the Federal authorities had gathered seventeen warships and sixty other vessels to carry the tons of supplies and matériel. In addition more than 12,500 soldiers had already been crammed aboard transport ships in dismal conditions for several weeks. This fleet, the largest ever assembled under the American flag up to that time, carried everything that would be needed to establish the base of operations at Port Royal.[5]

The Confederates were forewarned of Federal intentions through the Northern press. They knew the great fleet existed and would soon be somewhere on their coast, but they did not know for certain where it would strike. However, deductive reasoning on their part and reports of spies pointed to Port Royal Sound as the likely objective of the Federal operations.[6]

The Southerners had been in the process of fortifying their coast that summer, and by October, Port Royal Sound was well defended. On the north point of Hilton Head Island stood Fort Walker, a large sand fortification mounting twenty-three big cannons; across Port Royal Sound, on the southern end of St. Phillip's Island, was another sand fortification, Fort Beauregard, mounting nineteen guns. Fully armed, manned, and ready, the Confederate defenders watched and waited, confident that they could repel the expected invasion.[7]

For the residents of coastal Georgia, the war had seemed remote and distant through its early months, and they watched with pride as Southern hopes rose. Georgia took its stand for Southern independence in January 1861 by withdrawing from the Union. In Savannah state troops occupied Fort Pulaski, a massive brick fort at the mouth of the Savannah River, before Federal troops could garrison it and close the entrance to the river. Georgia troops quickly mustered, and some had even gone to Virginia to "illustrate" Georgia on the field of battle.

The news of Lincoln's blockade was received in Georgia with much ridicule, but on 31 May 1861 the steamer USS *Union* arrived off Savannah to blockade that port and Charleston. It had been chartered at Philadelphia five days after Lincoln's proclamation and was commanded by Capt. John R. Goldsborough.[8] The citizens of Savannah were not intimidated by this display of naval might at their doorstep in the form of the steamer *Union*. During the summer months of 1861 Confederate forces had been busily building sand batteries and fortifications on all the major offshore barrier islands along the Georgia coast to protect the entrances to the inland waterways. With the brick fortifications of Fort Pulaski as the northern anchor and with Fort Clinch on Cumberland Sound near Fernandina, Florida, as the southern anchor, this defense covered the entire Georgia coast. The sand batteries built on the islands between these two forts were constructed by slave labor gathered from the local plantations, and each battery mounted from two to five 32-pounder cannons. It was felt that these would be sufficient protection from nuisance raids similar to those executed by British vessels in the War of 1812.

For most Southern soldiers who garrisoned these lonely sand batteries, the war was something of a lark. Possessed of extreme patriotism, they were determined to repel any hostile moves against their defenses, but the tranquillity of their surroundings defied the fact that they were at war. Through the late summer and early autumn of 1861 they prepared for the fight they all knew must eventually come. But their enemy was more often nature and boredom rather than any mortal foe. Although the Southern men were ready and hopeful of engaging the enemy, the majority of their warfare at this time was practiced on an enemy of a different sort. Orderly Sergeant Walter A. Clark of the 63rd Georgia Infantry summed up this aspect best when he wrote in later years, "We fought and bled, it is true, but not on the firing line. The foes that troubled us most, were the fleas and sand flies and mosquitoes that infested that section. They never failed to open the spring campaign promptly and from their attacks at night and day no vigilance on the picket line could furnish even slight immunity. . . . Their bills were presented on the first day of the month, and, unfortunately, on every other day."[9]

Although Lincoln had put into effect the blockade of the Southern coast just five months earlier, its effects were being felt with higher prices and shortages of many things, particularly in such goods as medicines. A real awareness of what a blockade meant was dawning on the Southern people. Already merchant's shelves were taking on a bare look as goods were depleted with no hope of restocking them quickly. Corn was going for $1.20 a bushel in Savannah, while it cost 45 cents a bushel in New York. Pork was going for $27 a barrel in Savannah, but only for $15 a barrel in New York.[10] Items such as tea and coffee, once considered commonplace, quickly were becoming luxuries. Certain types of cloth, clothing, and leather goods also were becoming hard to find. Some items could not be found at all, while others were only available at highly inflated prices. The army demanded many items of necessity, such as salt, corn, meat, hats, and medicines, for example, and there was little left for the general markets. The only alternatives were to do without or to make do with what one had or could get.

While the blockade during this period was not nearly as effective as it would become, the U.S. Navy focused its efforts at specific ports, such as Wilmington, in North Carolina, Charleston, and Savannah, where ships had been successful in interdicting some shipping traffic. However, European countries such as Britain had not yet become actively involved in the business of blockade running. European merchants were willing to sell goods to Southern firms but generally left the transportation of these goods to the purchasers.

For the South much of the initial emphasis was on the government purchasing the military goods to feed its expanding military requirements. Since the South was not in the business of manufacturing large quantities of arms and accoutrements, it looked to European suppliers to meet these needs, and many European countries took this opportunity to unload large stocks of old, obsolete military goods on Southern buyers. For a time, consumer markets in the South were overlooked by Europeans. It did not take long for private individuals to recognize the profit potential in running the blockade to meet these consumer needs. But until the blockade running became better organized, the problems of shortages and high prices would continue.

The massive U.S. invasion fleet sailed onward toward Port Royal Sound. On the night of 31 October the fleet ran into heavy weather off Cape Hatteras. In the ensuing storm, four ships were lost, and the great fleet was scattered across fifty miles of ocean. Gradually the scattered fleet made its way toward the rendezvous point, about ten miles off Hilton Head Island, and by 4 November it had almost reassembled there.[11]

Heavy seas and high winds prevented the attack on 6 November, but on the seventh, the day dawned beautifully and clearly, bringing perfect weather over Port Royal Sound. About 8:30 A.M. the signal was given, and seventeen warships weighed anchor and proceeded in formation toward the sound. As they came in range, Confederate gunners opened fire. The battle for Port Royal Sound and Hilton Head Island had begun.[12] The thundering rumble of the big guns reverberated incessantly for miles along the coast as the residents of Georgia and South Carolina watched and waited confidently for news of the outcome. But the news was not good. The Confederate forces on Hilton Head suffered a resounding defeat, and U.S. troops were soon firmly established ashore. As this became known, a wave of uncertainty and panic swept across the coast, and some residents of Savannah fled the city in haste.

On 8 November the Federal expedition began unloading troops, supplies, and equipment for the conversion of Hilton Head Island into a vast supply depot and naval repair facility. For the Confederate authorities in Georgia, it did not take long for the lessons of the Port Royal disaster to sink in. The fortifications on the islands had been battered by overwhelming firepower from U.S. Navy warships, and it was only through a stroke of luck that the Confederate defenders had been able to avoid capture. The presence of Confederate gunboats and civilian vessels enabled the Confederate forces to leave the island. It was readily apparent that this debacle could easily be repeated by the Federal naval forces at any of the sand fortifications that had been constructed, armed, and manned on all of Georgia's major offshore islands that summer. The Southerners realized they did not have the means to defend these island batteries from the Federal forces, which could, at their convenience, cut off and capture any of these island batteries along with their garrisons and equipment. The Southerners might soon find themselves blockaded by their own batteries. This expenditure of troops, ordnance, and equipment could not be condoned, and a reevaluation of the coastal defensive strategy was needed.

Gen. Robert E. Lee, commander of the Department of South Carolina, Georgia, and East Florida, finally decided to abandon the major offshore islands and to focus the coastal defense only on points of major importance. Savannah was to be the only area defended in depth, and other areas along the coast where enemy troops might be landed would be closely guarded but not fortified. The Atlantic and Gulf Railroad, which ran between Savannah and Thomasville in the southwest corner of the state, could be used to concentrate troops rapidly at any threatened point. Lee immediately issued orders to abandon the offshore islands and emplace the guns in Savannah; the troops on the islands would be moved to mainland points that could be more adequately defended and supported.

Lee's orders affected more than the military establishments on those islands. The coastal planters also found themselves at risk of possible enemy harassment. With many plantations and summer homes scattered all over the exposed coastal mainland and offshore islands, most of these inhabitants began to close them up and move their stock, crops, and slaves to points of safety further inland.

On the evening of 12 November, the blockade runner *Fingal* approached the coast from Bermuda. Under the cover of darkness the ship slipped in toward Brunswick, Georgia, but found all the beacons and buoys blacked out. The vessel flashed a series of signals toward the darkened shoreline but received no response and steamed northward to see about getting into Savannah. In the end luck was with its crew, and they managed to slip into the Savannah River undetected. The cargo of arms, munitions, and military equipment was a valuable contribution to the Southern cause.

At Hilton Head Island the Federal forces were well on their way to establishing the vast support base there, so they were in no great hurry to mount further large-scale offensive operations. When they had assaulted Port Royal Sound, Savannah had been virtually unprepared to withstand an attack, but with the fall of Port Royal, Confederate authorities at Savannah wasted no time in taking defensive measures and massing troops to meet the threat. As time passed, it became evident that the Federals would be content with their hold on Hilton Head Island and not seriously threaten any other points. A sense of relief was felt as each passing day saw Southern defenses strengthened against the eventual attack that all felt was inevitable.

The additional gunboats brought south with the Port Royal expedition allowed the navy to extend the blockade. These vessels quickly spread out along the coast of Georgia and South Carolina, striving to enforce the blockade with more authority and effectiveness. It was an awesome task. The blockade runner *Fingal* had eluded them, but Federal officers vowed that the vessel would not slip past them again. However, there were some captures, as vigilant lookouts scanned the horizons and the blockading ships patrolled the offshore waters. Prior to the Port Royal operation the blockade generally consisted of vessels assigned to watch the approaches to specific ports, such as Charleston and Savannah. While this method had been effective to a degree, it proved difficult to close these ports completely.

Following the establishment of the Federal base at Port Royal Sound and Hilton Head Island, blockading vessels patrolled the offshore waters, alert for ships attempting an approach to the southeast coast. In some instances legitimate merchant vessels heading for ports further south could be found too close to the coast. When sighted, these ships were challenged. If they attempted to elude the blockaders, they were pursued and overtaken if possible. If they heaved to when challenged and allowed themselves to be boarded and their papers checked, they were usually warned and released. This helped prevent unpleasant incidents, as more than one Federal supply vessel was challenged and overtaken as a suspected blockade runner, only to find that their cargoes were destined for the support of Federal operations and not for Southern ports.

The profits to be made from running the blockade attracted many people, one of whom was forty-year-old Thomas L. Hernandez, a resident of Savannah who was a river pilot and well acquainted with the coastal waterways of Georgia. Not much is known of his early life. He and his brothers and sister were from St. Augustine, Florida, but the family had relocated to Savannah, where they settled. Hernandez was married to Maryann C. (Lamstad) Cazier, thirty-two, a native of Cecil County, Maryland. She had been married previously and had a daughter, Isabella. The couple was married in 1845 and had four children of their own, three boys and a girl, ranging in ages from two to fourteen in 1861.[13]

When the war broke out, Hernandez initially enlisted as a private in the Phoenix Riflemen, Capt. George A. Gordon's company of the 1st Georgia Infantry. Hernandez later transferred to Company C of

Thomas L. Hernandez, photographed during his imprisonment in Fort Warren, Boston Harbor, in 1864. Courtesy of Ms. Nancy Pelletier.

the 13th Battalion, Georgia Infantry, but he soon found himself on detached service since there was a need for river pilots who could bring the blockade-runners safely into port.[14] With his intimate knowledge of the coastal waters, it was no surprise that his talents were utilized. In late November he was aboard the schooner *Albion,* heading for the South Carolina coast. The *Albion,* built in Maryland, was commanded by Capt. Luke Christy, fifty-one, of Savannah, former captain of the tugboat *Lamar.*[15]

Flying the English flag, the *Albion* departed Nassau, Bahamas, with a cargo of fruit, shoes, saddles, bridles, salt, and other goods greatly in demand on Southern commercial and military markets. On the afternoon of 25 November 1861, as the *Albion* approached the offshore waters of the North Edisto River below Charleston, it was sighted by the blockader USS *St. Lawrence.* The ship approached and warned the *Albion* to put about and vacate the area, which it promptly did. The *Albion* then maneuvered to make another attempt from a different approach when it was sighted by the blockader USS *Penguin,* which immediately set off in pursuit.[16]

After an hour's chase, the *Penguin* caught the schooner and took it into custody. On questioning, Captain Christy reported that he was from Nova Scotia, but later, aboard the USS *Susquehanna,* a Federal naval officer recognized one of the *Albion*'s crew members as an old schoolmate from Savannah. It then came out that the entire crew was from that city. A prize crew was put aboard the *Albion,* which, with its crew, passengers, and cargo, was sent to New York City for disposition.[17] With Tom Hernandez on his way to New York City, everything was in place for the beginning of his story of adventure and misadventure. Events would move quickly once he reached New York.

TWO

Bound for Nova Scotia

om Hernandez and those captured aboard the blockade runner *Albion* off Charleston arrived in New York City on 1 December 1861. After two weeks the case was disposed of, with the vessel and cargo being auctioned and its crew and passengers released or incarcerated, as circumstances dictated. Since Hernandez was probably considered to be a civilian noncombatant, he was subsequently released and may have been warned by officials about being caught again aboard a ship full of contraband cargo too close to the Southern coast.

In the intervening time Hernandez made his way to neighboring Newark, New Jersey, to visit the family of James Dickson Sr.—friends from Savannah. Dickson had lived for many years in Savannah, where he operated a dry goods and confectionary store on Broughton Street. Eventually he established a business in Newark, where the family resided for a portion of each year. However, by 1860 the Dicksons had apparently settled in Newark on a more permanent basis as the Savannah City Directory for 1860 notes only James Dickson Sr. as a resident boarding at the Marshall House. The outbreak of the war found them living at their Newark residence, and because of the press of events, they remained there.[1]

When Tom Hernandez arrived at the Dickson residence at 1 Washington Place, he found Mr. and Mrs. Dickson at home with their twenty-five-year-old son, James Jr., and the family's domestic servant, Bridget Larman. Bridget, a twenty-two-year-old emigrant from

Ireland, had been employed by the family for only a short time. The Dickson home was situated at the end of a street only two blocks long, across from which was located Washington Park, a spacious triangular-shaped park filled with large elm trees and various monuments.[2]

Young James apparently had not yielded to the first calls for troops, but his sympathies must have been with his brothers in the South. He probably stayed in Newark to assist his father in the business, but he must have kept a sharp eye on the developing events near his native Savannah. The war had affected his father's business sharply by cutting off the markets in Savannah, and James was probably anxious to take some active part in the conflict before it was resolved. Tom Hernandez was likely quite vocal about his recent exploits and adventures in running the blockade and about the quick profit that could be made while doing it. He may have declared his intentions to continue these activities and even encouraged young James to join him since he knew that James had prior experience working on merchant vessels, which would be of value in any blockade-running venture.

On the evening of 16 December, Hernandez and James Dickson Jr. traveled to the Jersey City docks on the Hudson River, where they arranged with Capt. William Stephens of the British brigantine *Lilly Dale* to take them up the Bay of Fundy to Nova Scotia. They worked as crewmen to pay for their passage. The *Lilly Dale* was a two-masted sailing vessel, ninety-four feet long with a twenty-four-foot beam, drawing eleven and a half feet of water and weighing 176 tons. The vessel had been built at the famed E. C. Churchill and Sons shipyards at Hantsport, Nova Scotia, in 1858 and launched the following spring.[3]

The Dicksons had family and friends at Halifax, Nova Scotia. James's uncles, William and Peter Donaldson, resided on adjoining estates at Birch Cove, about six miles northwest of Halifax. Peter Donaldson and his wife Susannah had eight children, six girls and two boys. James and his family had often visited the Donaldsons in years past.[4] Dickson and Hernandez knew they could easily board a blockade runner in Halifax or obtain passage to Bermuda or Nassau if necessary. They were all set to depart on the following morning at 7:00 A.M. Dickson knew he was about to embark on a great adventure, and he began to keep a diary to record the events.

The early morning of 17 December was cold and clear at Newark, and Dickson and Hernandez were up before daylight making final preparations. Dickson recorded the first entry in his diary: "With a sad heart and many regrets I tore myself from (   )⁵ Parting is always sad. I was undertaking at best a perilous adventure at a most inclement season of the year leaving the most affectionate of Mothers behind me, not knowing when I should again be enabled to meet her. My parting I may add was particularly painful rendered so by the many peculiar circumstances surrounding me."⁶

After a quick breakfast, Dickson and Hernandez gathered their bags, bundled up against the chilly December air, and prepared for the short trek to the Jersey City docks. It was still dark when they departed. "A hasty farewell, a Mother's blessing and we were off with my baggage on our shoulders. The moon was throwing its lengthened shadows down Washington Place. The stately old elm trees in the park stood out like grim spectors in the silent ghost-like scenes. The keen frosty air of a December morning caused us to quicken our paces, and as we turned the <u>old corner</u> I lost sight of that which contained what was most dear to me."

Hernandez and Dickson made their way through the streets of Newark as the pinkish light of dawn crept across the chilly horizon. By sunrise they were dockside in Jersey City, where the *Lilly Dale* was preparing to depart. Once they were aboard, Captain Stephens wasted no time in casting off the lines, and the *Lilly Dale* eased away from the dock. Dickson wrote, "On board the brig at seven, hauling into the stream of the Jersey City ferry house, boats passing and re-passing every few minutes under our stern. Awaiting our pilot and the 'water boat.'"

Dickson and Hernandez went below to stow their baggage but found that their accommodations were to be rather sparse. Dickson wrote, "Our little cooped up box of a cabin was well packed with three passengers, skipper, [first] mate and cook, with two chests, a small table and a stove. Oh that stove. All in a space eight [feet] by twelve [feet]. . . . As our pretty craft, the LILLY DALE, was not often honored with a list of three passengers on her list of passengers, [and] as we had been however previously informed, found no bedding, but an empty bunk which we might rig out as comfortable as our limited means would allow. A stray bit of new canvas about a fathom long was spread out as a mattress, carpet bag for a pillow, overcoat and shawl for blankets and coverlet and a felt hat for my night cap and that for the voyage."

The *Lilly Dale* spent the better part of the day at anchor in the Hudson River, waiting for a pilot. It was 3:00 P.M. when Dickson noted, "Water boat along side and Pilot on board. Weighed anchor and stood down with the ebb [tide] to the Battery, made sail and ran up with the East River flood [tide] through 'Hell-gate.'" Once the *Lilly Dale* passed through the Hell Gate, the channel began to widen as the East River opened into the back reaches of Long Island Sound. Once beyond Riker's Island, Captain Stephens ordered the vessel anchored off the Revenue Cutter as the daylight hours waned. That evening aboard the *Lilly Dale,* Dickson recorded another entry in his diary at 10:00 P.M.:

Anchored a few hundred yards from the Revenue Cutter. Her beautiful low, black piratical looking hull, her fine tapering masts, well braced yards and taut rigging, formed a perfect picture on the blue bespangled horizon, lit as bright as day by the silvery rays of the moon. We could not go to sea without our papers being examined and found correct, as all vessels after sunset bound in or out were compelled to anchor until daylight under her guns. All passengers were prohibited from leaving without a "pass-port" signed by the Sec. of State, foreigners to get certificates from the ministers of their respective Governments, citizens to take the oath of allegiance before the proper authorities. To prevent any violation of this law all passengers before going on board of vessels had to produce their certificate of departure to police officers stationed at their gangways on the eve of departure; and at the [Verrazano] "Narrows" and below "Hell-gate" each had its respective Cutter on the alert to overhaul every craft bound in or out, examine papers, question the Captain if desirable to the officers and detain her and make a thorough search if necessary.

For Dickson and Hernandez, their first solid meal aboard the *Lilly Dale* was an event worthy of the adventure they were about to undertake. Dickson wrote, "Meals, whenever they could be cooked, consisted of coffee that would forever cure the Parisean from indulging in that beverage again, served in pint cups with distorted representation of some unknown formation in the flowery kingdom painted in glaring colors of red, yellow and green on the outside; a fine dish for the select party of Eskimos, consisting of salt fat pork and salt cod fish minced and then fried in a sea of essential oil of hog. Our bread [was] a compound of which even our stomach was bound to give way to at last, a yellow looking stuff made of Saleratus and flour, sometimes better, sometimes worse, according to accident or the weather; but no sauce like a sharp appetite and salt water."

The following morning, 18 December, the crew made final preparations aboard ship before their departure. Dickson and Hernandez had signed on to work for their passage, but since they were leaving the country illegally, they had to wait until the vessel had been inspected and cleared by Customs officials aboard the revenue cutter before taking their place with the crew. Dickson recorded in his diary:

The wind veered during the night to the eastward, consequently [we] did not weigh anchor before 2 P.M. on the 18th. On our making sail to run down to the "Cutter" we went below concealing ourselves in the forecastle chock forward in the smallest imaginable space amongst oil cloths, coal and rope coils in a gloomy state of uncertainty in regards to our getting on British soil.

As we ran down to the Cutter we could hear the noise above on deck as the top-sail was hauled aback. Our dark subterranean hiding place, redolent with tar, bilge water, and murderous volumes of black and sulphurous vapors from the bituminous compound on fire in a small cracked stove which at variance to all scientific law and well regulated stove pipes, would belch out in dense black clouds through every crack and bars of the grate instead of ascending in those spiral curves and float into the blue sky above us. Amidst all our conflicting emotions we knew our position to be sublimely ridiculous and we certainly felt it if we could not appreciate it.

After a delay of some fifteen minutes, another rumpus on deck, ["]yeo, heave yeo!,["] followed in a deep powerful voice "belay." Then a musical sound as the water rippled, splashed and splurged against our bows. We certainly felt more comfortable as we knew we were again "under-weigh." Our skipper, a huge specimen from Nova Scotia, half codfish kind of fellow, put his bullet head, encased in a huge Seal Skin Cap, down the companion way and roared out "All right now."

On reaching the deck our brig had nearly all canvas set bowling off her seven knots and leaving the Cutter fast astern. Fort Schuyler on our port-quarter guarding the entrance up to the "City" by the Sound. A regiment of Zouaves were marching through its massive granite gate-ways. A good swig from our flasks tended materially to restore our nerves and at the same time wash the coating of soot from our throats.

The *Lilly Dale* proceeded on a northeasterly course sailing through Long Island Sound toward the reaches of Cape Cod Spit. It was cold and brisk on the rolling and rough open water. Dickson continued his narrative on 20 December after they had come to anchor off Cape Cod in a harbor on the north side of Martha's Vineyard. He recorded, "On the morning of the 20th we dropped anchor in 'Holmes Hole.' The usual amount of vessels weather bound were riding at anchor. The 'bum boat' with <u>Sea pies</u> and newspapers came alongside. The weather was blowing and thick, threatening snow. After an hours delay it was thought prudent enough to continue our voyage and [we were] soon leaving the light house astern and threading the intricate and now dangerous passage of 'Nantucket Shoals.' . . . Weather getting gradually worse and worse. Everything all snug on board the 'Lilly Dale' only anxious that we may be enabled to eat Christmas dinner on shore."

For the next few days, the *Lilly Dale* continued to pick its way through the gale-tossed seas, heading northeast, up the coast of Maine. On 23 December, as the ship was plunging through another driving gale on the stormy North Atlantic, Dickson took a few moments to make an entry in his diary. "Again lying to under close reefed main-sail and main stay sail with [the] wheel lashed. All hands below. Blowing heavily from the Southwest with dringing storm of snow, sleet and rain. Brig rolling fearfully. . . . The stove in our <u>rat hole</u>, as we term it, takes queer notions and frequently drives us up the companionway and even on deck amidst the driving spray and snow for fresh air; however we have our jokes and they are enjoyed with a relish by even the cook at whose expense they are often cracked. During the night all hands in the cabin set to work making reefing points to balance the mainsail." The *Lilly Dale* sailed onward while its crew spent the hours sewing up reefing points, which were reinforced holes in the canvas where ropes could be tied. On 24 December the storm let up but showed no signs of breaking. Dickson recorded some of the day's events aboard ship.

"Christmas-eve" This morning [we] lost our breakfast and the "main-stay-sail." Poor old cook has been rather imprudent in eating too freely of his "duff" imitating no doubt the example of the Royal Beef-eaters of old, by way of restoring the confidence of all hands on board as to the sanitary qualities of his Bread. Consequently [the] Cook is laid up, [with] a severe indisposition somewhere in the gastric regions.

Weather no better, worse if anything. Brig doing nobly. Skipper has at last given up the chart as a conglomeration of admiralty hylerglypics [sic], thrown his dead reckoning overboard and comes no doubt to the conclusion that "nobody knows where we are."

After the remains of yesterdays meals had been eaten for our dinner it was decided that it wouldn't do to allow the cook to remain any longer in his bunk if it was even necessary for him to swallow the Medicine Chest. Castor Oil, Rhubarb, Jalap each had its advocates. After due perusal of the Seamans Medical Directory it was gravely asserted in the presence of the victim that it was absolutely necessary to make a compound of the three articles so well known, that he would then receive the full benefit peculiar to each of the above medicines, and taken together his complaint and his pain must certainly give way.

After a due amount of assertions from us and bullying and swearing from the [first] mate [the Cook] was induced to take it. As we all knew he was now "hors de combat," for some time at least a new cook had to be appointed. Major, a florid complexioned bluff sailor boy from Hants[port] was taken from the forecastle and duly installed as Commander in Chief in the brig's galley.

Christmas Day was cold and unsettled at sea aboard the *Lilly Dale*. Dickson wrote,

Christmas morning. Blowing fearful. Major had made many attempts before succeeding in getting the galley fires lit. At last [he] makes his appearance, a dish of potatoes in one hand and herrings in the other making many queer movements to retain his center of gravity and with much skill and some assistance places the dishes before us with the prudential advice "each fellow look out for himself. Lee side keep a sharp eye to windward and the Coffee-pot."

William Crowell, the [first] mate, a hardy, honest specimen of the British Sailor enveloped in oil cloth and Sou-wester is like a huge Newfoundland dog as he shakes the water from him and appears in his element in the fearful weather and gives us a not very favorable opinion of a speedy change in the weather.

Interesting group in our little 8 x 12 cabin floor. Weather intensely cold, cannot get [a] fire to burn in [the] cabin [stove], bunks getting wet, sundry ingenious plans devised to turn off the water.

That night Dickson recorded another entry.

Night has again set in at 4, and no day light for sixteen hours and the gale continues with unabated fury and to make matters worse, on a <u>lee-shore</u>. Fearful weather and [make] no mistake. We all feel very anxious, however God can protect us here as on land. . . .

Occasionally a sea breaks over our sides with a heavy thump, rattling and pitching everything moveable about. What a fearful yet grand sight with-all, our gallant little craft struggling with the sea. How she rises to meet that fearful sea as it come thundering and surging down on us seemingly to engulf us and as it sweeps by only to rise to the succeeding wave as it comes angrily onward following in fearful rapidity the preceding masses of water.

And here we are on this world of waters, a single lantern burning in our weather rigging and but one [man] on deck and he lashed to the wheel, uncertain at what moment a sea may come on board and swamp us. But she comes well up to the sea and is not heavily laden and we trust in Providence and turn in for the night. So ends Christmas day. May the Dear ones I have left, have had indeed a Merry Christmas on shore and know nought of our discomforts.

The gale raging across the North Atlantic began to moderate during Christmas night and by the morning of 26 December the *Lilly Dale* was making better time. Dickson wrote, "Weather more moderate. Sea gone down considerable. [We] made sail about 9 A.M. The Cunard steamer carrying the Royal mail passed about four miles to windward of us. [We] knew at once we were further southward than [we] had anticipated, also to the eastward of calculation. Fortunately during the day [the] wind sprung up from the eastward nearly a gale. [We] ran before it with single reefed mainsail, the log showing II, II½ and sometimes I2 knots. Running into the westward to make 'Mount Desert Rock' [Maine]. Blowing a close reef-top sail breeze all night. Toward day light [we] hauled more up to the nor'ward, weather thick and raining; kept a sharp lookout forward."

By the morning of 27 December the men of the *Lilly Dale* found the sailing a little easier as the gale apparently subsided. Their position was calculated to be somewhere off of Penobscot Bay along the rocky coast of Maine. Dickson recorded, "About 9:00 A.M. Land dead ahead from the top-sail-yard. Veered away [and] sent [the first] mate aloft. [He] thought it [was] 'Long Island.' [We] ran up the coast close hauled, 'weather looking dirty.' We could now see the rock-bound coast of Maine, the sea rolling in with immense force and breaking on the rocks within half a mile of us throwing the spray in silver clouds to a great height. Soon 'Baker Island Light' looms up through the haze."

The Baker Island Light was a welcome sight to those aboard the *Lilly Dale* as it pointed the way to Frenchman's Bay, where they could find a sheltered anchorage from the threatening weather. The coastline of Maine loomed through the haze along the western horizon, showing rounded, rocky summits covered with snow and the mottled green of fir forests scattered along the shores. The mounded summits of Mount Desert Island dominated the coastal profile. Dickson continued his narrative:

> We ran well to the nor'ward before we stand in. "Mount Desert Rock" rises up from the sea covered with snow; we soon drop anchor in the harbor or rather Bay under [the] lee of Mount Desert and off one of the Cranberry Islands. What a pleasing sound as our anchor drops from the "Cat-heads" rattling the chain cable like lightning after it through the "hawser-hole."
>
> After dinner [we] man the boat. Lower into her the water cask to be filled on shore (only a few gallons left on board) a hastily written letter thrust into my overcoat pocket, my mackintosh well secured I was soon over the sides [and] into the boat below. What visions of fresh eggs, butter, fresh beef run through my head though only ten days out.

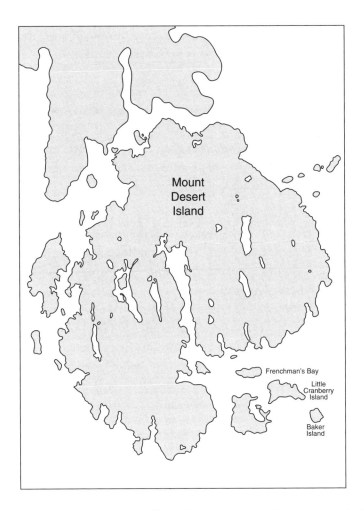

Mount Desert Island

Frenchman's Bay

Little Cranberry Island

Baker Island

Whilst the crew are filling the cask from a short way up the beach I cross over to a fisherman's house about a mile distant through the now fast freezing snow and slush. A tall robust looking young fellow hails me with "Won't you come in out [of] the cold?" With thanks I hand him my letter and was told it would leave with the mail the next day for the mainland, 26 miles distant. I got eight fine, fat wild ducks for 80 cents and for a few cents more I got my pockets well filled with onions and several [news]papers of last week. Of course the boat's crew said I had done a big thing.

We shoved off for the <u>Lilly</u> about sun-set. How changed was everything. The snow to the nor'west was tinged like gold with the rays of the setting sun. Our beautiful brig of 170 tons lay some two miles out in the Bay quietly riding at anchor. The cold air s[w]eeping down from the mountains across the bay too plainly told us the wind [was] dead ahead.

As we came alongside [the *Lilly*] the cook hailed me or rather the bunch of ducks with evident satisfaction however the old fellow proclaimed me as public benefactor. What a jolly mess we all hands had that night, a conglomerate mass of Salt Pork, wild duck, dough, turnips, potatoes and onions made a splendid "Lobs-sconce" for cabin and fore castle.

With the weather changing for the worst again, the men battened the hatches and prepared to ride out the storm for the night. At 8:00 P.M. that night Dickson recorded, "Wind rapidly increasing. Ran out the full length of [anchor] cable, 125 fathoms, and prepared to let go the best bower. 8 bells. Let go the best bower and 90 fathoms chain. Cautioned the anchor watch to keep a sharp lookout in case she dragged any, and if things got any worse to call all hands up. Heavy sea running, temperature dreadfully cold and the wind howling through our rigging fearfully. As she comes up to the sea it jerks her severely and there is no doubt but she is straining considerably. Turn into our bunks and almost wish ourselves at sea again instead [of] riding out the gale at anchor in 'Frenchmans Bay.'"

The series of gales continued to batter the area with high winds, snow, freezing rain, and rough seas that increased as the night progressed. The men rode out the storm as best they could, but by 4:00 A.M. the following morning they found their situation steadily deteriorating. Then the man on deck sounded the alarm. Dickson recorded,

All hands roused up on deck. Brig dragging her anchors and fast going ashore and no help for it. Nothing could be done. [We] kept "lead" agoing, [water] gradually shoaling. At daylight found we were within 200 yards of the beach about a mile above the "Fish-house." A schooner which had run in, for shelter like ourselves the previous evening and had anchored near us was lying on the beach her top-masts gone and the sea going right over her. Her rigging was one solid mass of ice; the wind was blowing now a perfect hurricane, breaking of[f] the tops of the seas and sweeping them across the "bay" in one complete sheet of foam and spray. Every sea that would break forward, the moment it struck the rigging or deck would instantly become ice, in fact we were encased in ice, our sides, every yard, even our sails froze solid. The people [on shore] were launching a boat evidently to the wrecked schooner.

In a few minutes our stern post struck [the bottom] with a shock nearly throwing us off our feet as she came down in the trough of the sea. We kept thumping and driving up the beach afraid of our top masts coming down on deck, however the tide had now turned and was fast ebbing and with a rise and fall here of nearly twenty feet, at low water we should be high and dry and would walk ashore; but on the flood [tide] it was evident our brig would go to pieces. Everything was got ready in case of such [an] event. Men's chests [were] packed, charts, papers, colors, quadrants, etc. secured. After a few hours pounding and scraping over the rocky beach we were on land instead of water.

With the ship firmly grounded, Dickson and Hernandez bundled up and went ashore to see if they could contact the local inhabitants. Dickson continued,

A most severe and fatiguing walk on the ice, the wind blowing us in an opposite direction from that in which we were bound; falls, bruises; and [cold] benumbing our feet, hands, ears and nose freezing with an intensity perfectly Arctic, we managed to get under shelter of a small clump of woods from which we soon gained the first fisherman's house. The partly insensible, frozen and benumbed crew of the Yankee coaster had been conveyed here and were being kindly cared for. Poor wretches, they looked pitiful. They had saved what they stood in and all were more or less badly frozen when taken ashore.

They had parted their cable during the night [and] drove over a ledge of rocks tearing an immense hole in the schooner's bottom. She was loaded with wood, and soon became water logged. They took refuge in the cabin filled with water rapidly turning into ice. [T]heir efforts to keep up animation was the only thing that had kept them alive during the fearful night. It was a sad scene and but too frequent at this season of the year on this wild coast.

We crossed about a quarter of a mile further to a wrecker's house. [We met] a young couple who treated us with much kindness. A fine hearty supper spread on the whitest of linen and served in the holiday china from the hands of a charming young wife, the lady of our host, made us soon forget our troubles and misfortunes. That night Tom and I helped them make up the best bed in the parlor and slept as sweetly and soundly as if we had been at home instead of the wrecker's house on Cranberry Island.

The winter storm continued to rage across the coast of Maine during the night and into the morning of 29 December. On Cranberry Island, Dickson and Hernandez were up early preparing to return to the stranded *Lilly Dale*. They hoped it would be possible to save the vessel from being pounded to pieces by the incoming tide and somehow get the ship back into deep water. Dickson wrote,

Sunday morning blowing heavy still from the nor'west but evidently moderating. The "lulls" are more frequent and seem to last longer.

View from Little Cranberry Island, with Mount Desert Rock seen in the distance. Frenchman's Bay is in the foreground. This stretch of rocky beach is believed to be the place where the Lilly Dale was driven ashore on the morning of 27 December 1861. Many ships have suffered the same fate over the years, and a ledge of rocks, just off the white buildings seen at distant center, has brought others to grief. This would have been where Dickson and his comrades witnessed another ship breaking apart on the rocks near the shore. Photograph by the author.

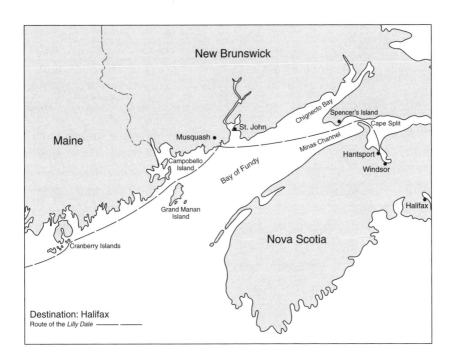

Destination: Halifax
Route of the *Lilly Dale* —— ——

Our breakfast was as choice and abundant as our previous supper. The brig we understood was in the position she was the day before. After a hearty dinner the skipper sent for us. The gale was going down fast and at 12 that night we would attempt to "warp" out on "full-flood" [tide].

Paying 87 cents apiece, the amount of charges, we were soon down the beach and on board the brig. They had been very comfortable on board during the night all hands being housed below except the [deck] watch which was changed every 20 minutes to keep him from freezing. Think of that ye grumblers when the thermometers stand at 98 in the shade. Sunday night we all hands worked on the windlass, lights burning in the "fore-rigging." We warped her out during Monday [morning] into deep water.

After getting the vessel off the Cranberry Island beach, the crew brought it to anchor in deep water once again and turned in for a well-earned rest. By the early morning light of 30 December they inspected the ship and found it none the worse for its beaching, and later in the day they weighed anchor, set sail, and headed up the coast.

Bound for Nova Scotia

The morning of 31 December found the *Lilly Dale* sailing easily along the coast of Maine and approaching the coast of New Brunswick, Canada. The weather was with the crew, but no one knew how long it would last, as the winter season in the northeast is a time when fine sailing weather is the exception and not the rule. Dickson recorded,

Sun rose in all its splendor, the wind from the south-west and all hands in high glee. Even the old cook ceases to grumble about his stove-pipe. All smiles, he makes his appearance with coffee pot in [his] hands, compliments all hands and praises the brig and makes known his determination to put on a clean shirt and wash his hands, and hopes to God he'll be with his missus and eat his New Years dinner at home.

We have a beautiful run up the coast running sometimes within a few hundred feet of the high picturesque headlands. Occasionally some fisherman bound in or out passes our bows. As we gradually overhaul some coaster bound in, up and [we] have him astern. The blue sea seems be-sprinkled with white sails. As we run up, before sunset, the "Grand Manans" looms up over the starboard quarter and that is the commencement on this side of the bay of Her Majesty's territory of British America. It is certainly a grand appearance, its steep red cliffs covered with dense foliage of spruce and hemaetas, rising almost perpendicular from the water.

Here at different seasons of the year you will meet scores of birch bark canoes dancing over the waves, the Micmacs spearing fish, and porpoises. Camp-Bello [Island] is now off the port bow on the New Brunswick [border] Line. When the sun went down it unfortunately took the wind with it. As we turn in, an ebb tide is setting against us. No cheering thing even in the mouth of the "Bay of Fundy" and we think of home; that this is New Years eve at sea. All in a life-time; New Years may be another Christmas, who knows, as they say fine weather is short lived here at this season.

New Years Day found the *Lilly Dale* in the Bay of Fundy, forging ahead through rising seas and another winter gale. Dickson wrote in his diary,

New Years morning 1862—Blowing nearly dead ahead, another gale fast rising. . . . Battening down the hatches, weather getting thick.

Sixteen miles [south] of St. John's, [turn] about ship at 8:00 A.M. and run before the gale to make a harbor run into "Musquasch" before a driving squall of snow and sleet. . . .

This like nearly all the harbors on this coast is merely a cove or inlet from the sea. The cold, rugged snow covered hills rising several hundred feet above the water with only two or three newly erected huts on their sides to indicate its being inhabited. . . . With both anchors and all our chain out, yards sent down from aloft and [we] prepare to make the most of a bad job. Our New Years was spent gloomily enough.

On 2 January, they rode out another winter gale while safely anchored at Musquash. There was not much to do aboard ship except to keep a close eye on the storm and the vessel and keep warm and dry below deck. Dickson recorded, "It blew and snowed all day Thursday and night followed blowing and snowing and was spent pretty much in the same manner as New Years [with] Hard-tack and Salt Pork, Salt Pork and Hard tack."

On the morning of 3 January, the gale continued to blow with a heavy sea running. Aboard the *Lilly Dale,* they discussed whether or not to take the vessel out, when they saw a sight that stirred them to action. It was the *Queen of Clippers,* a two-masted schooner out of Windsor, Nova Scotia, passing offshore.[7] The sight of the *Queen,* plunging across the rolling seas with all sail set, was one that brought the crew of the *Lilly Dale* to their feet. Dickson wrote,

The "Queen" a beautiful clipper schooner of Windsor, Nova Scotia passed the offing running before this with "balanced reef main sail" set. This was too much for the crew of the "Lilly Dale," one of "the" cracked vessels [from] up "the Bay," "who considered it as a challenge to the Lilly and her crew." Ere long a roaring sea song burst on the gale as we weighed anchor.

We soon ran out, but we struggled with the gale, bounding on to our destined port. Here we had an opportunity of seeing not only the skill with which these hardy Scotians handle their vessels; but the seeming instinct they all possess of knowing their exact position on the chart by dead reckoning. We would clear reef, run off headlands, go between islands, [and] weather capes on one of the most dangerous coasts in the world in a gale without being able hardly to discern through the snow and mists our own "gib-boom end."

The *Lilly* plunged onward throughout the day with no sign of the gale letting up, but the gallant little vessel handled it well. The ship proceeded along the New Brunswick coast, past St. John, and into the Bay of Fundy. To the northeast of St. John, the Bay of Fundy splits into two bays. One, Chignecto Bay, continues northeasterly and the other, Cobequid Bay, bears off due east. With the gale pounding them relentlessly, the men aboard the *Lilly Dale* decided to make for the entrance of Cobequid Bay. About 9:00 P.M. that night, Dickson added to his diary entry: "It was considered prudent not to make for the passage called the Gut; but to run for Spencer's Island and make a lee of it all night."

About an hour later they left the Bay of Fundy, entered Minas Channel, and came to anchor in a small inlet on the north shore of the channel, known as Spencer's Bay, off a small, rocky outcropping called Spencer's Island. Once the vessel was securely battened down for the night, Dickson added a brief notation to his previous entry: "Again riding at anchor. Terrible night."

The winter storms still blew heavily across the Bay of Fundy when the morning of 4 January arrived on Nova Scotia's shores, but there was much anticipation aboard the *Lilly Dale* as the crew expected to reach their destination on this day if all went well. With the first gray light of morning, they weighed anchor and proceeded from Spencer's Bay into Minas Channel, which led into Cobequid Bay. They sailed eastward, toward a large, flat-topped strip of land that jutted abruptly into the bay from the south shore. At the point of this peninsula was Cape Split. On the other side was Hantsport, their destination. Dickson recorded, "7 A.M.—Again running up. The wind more moderate. Began to strike masses of ice. Cape Split, one of the wildest and most singular spots imaginable on the 'weather bow.' It is a mass of rock which has become by continued action of the waves against it for ages severed from the adjoining cliffs and rises in a single spire from the water. From here to Cape 'Blowmedown' the passage is very narrow and our brig could hardly keep steerage way for the currents which frequently runs 12 miles an hour."

Once the *Lilly Dale* passed Cape Split, the ship proceeded along the south shore of the flat-topped peninsula known as Cape Blomidon. Within an hour it had passed Blomidon, entered Minas Basin, and changed to a southerly course bound for the entrance of the Windsor River and Hantsport. Dickson returned to his diary and recorded an additional entry. "We are driving on now with the tide and wind and by 2 P.M., amidst a driving snow storm, drop anchor in Windsor River off 'Hantsport.' . . . I went in the boat that took the hawser on shore. At the 'Smithup' we were welcomed as lost sheep, many having given us up. We were the last vessel in and had not been reported since we left New York, now 19 days out. Mason and Slidell, had been demanded by the British Government and had been returned under the protecting folds of the Red Cross of St. George. Troops were pouring into the provinces, the Canadas, New Brunswick, Nova Scotia, Prince Edward [Island] had broken out in patriotic ardor and even New Foundland was volunteering for the Royal Navy."

Cape Split in Minas Bay, Nova Scotia. The Lilly Dale *passed here on the morning of 4 January 1862 on the way to Hantsport. The view here is to the south. Dickson noted that it was "one of the wildest and most singular spots imaginable." Photograph by the author.*

The E. C. Churchill shipyard at Hantsport, appearing much the way it did to Dickson and Hernandez when they landed nearby. Courtesy of the Nova Scotia Archives and Records Management.

The rolling countryside was thickly carpeted with a blanket of snow. Dickson made arrangements for a tiny, horse-drawn sleigh to carry them the four miles to Windsor, located just south of Hantsport. From Windsor they could obtain railroad connections to Halifax, about forty miles beyond. Their baggage was loaded aboard the sleigh, and they bid farewell to their companions from the *Lilly Dale*. Dickson continued his narrative: "We were soon stowed away amidst, baggage and furs, in a one seat shay, our reckless but withal skillful driver, was perched up between us. Our horses were driven tandem, let me say, the prettiest way of driving in the world. Thoroughly sportsman like. Away we went the moment the hosteler let go the leader, at a regular breakneck pace, across fields at times to avoid the drifts in the road. It was pleasant and had even a charm about it, that ride, which under other circumstances would have been perfectly delightful, as ladies would exclaim. As it was, our anxiety to reach Halifax that night made us insensible to all other feelings."

The horse-drawn sleigh made good time as it sped through the snowy countryside. Rolling hills and snowbound farms passed by quickly as the four miles separating Hantsport and Windsor disappeared beneath the horses' hooves and the runners of the sleigh. In a short time the travelers crossed over a low ridge, and the little city of Windsor came into view across a flat plain beside the Avon River. They came down the opposite side of the ridge and approached the Avon River Bridge, a long, covered wood bridge built in 1836. Their driver brought the sleigh to a halt beside the booth at the head of the bridge, where they paid the 25-cent toll for carriages.[8]

They were running late and in danger of missing the last train to Halifax, which would mean a delay in their plans to arrive at their destination before nightfall. Dickson continued, "We were soon rapidly crossing 'Avon Bridge' and in the pretty and thriving town of Windsor, a few minutes too late [to catch the train] which compelled us to wait until Monday, as very rightly, no trains were run over the [rail]road on Sunday."

There was little sense in trying to cross the forty miles of snowbound, rocky countryside between Windsor and Halifax by sleigh. They knew they would have to find accommodations in Windsor. Dickson suggested that they go to the Acadia House on the corner of Stannus and Gray streets, a few blocks away from the railroad depot. The owner, John Collins, a friend of the Dickson and Donaldson families, had purchased the Acadia House in 1852. Collins renovated the large frame building with an attached livery and operated it as a boarding house for private residents and travelers.[9]

Dickson and Hernandez went up the snowy streets where bare, overhanging limbs from the trees lining the walks provided a canopy above them. In a few moments they were in front of the Acadia House, unloaded their baggage and sought the warmth within. Dickson continued, "My old friend 'Collins' at once welcomed me and made me at home in his comfortable 'Inn.' As we place our feet on the warm hearth before the bright cheerful fire of 'Sydney Coal' in the cosily furnished apartment, illumed the now darkening room, and as we smile at the well polished poker, knowingly placed against the bars of the grate and pointing most mysteriously up the chimney, enters banchos ghost with tray and glasses from which is a most refreshing odor.

'Ale 'ot gentlemen,' says our landlord as we look suspiciously on this fleeting bit of lemon. Let me recommend, as an old traveler, 'Collins Inn' for a white linen, a well supplied table and a good glass of English ale and a pleasant, agreeable landlord who almost anticipates your very wishes."

On 5 January, James Dickson and Tom Hernandez spent a restful day at Collins's Acadia House. After two weeks of cold, high seas and winter gales, it must have been a relief to be back on solid ground. The following morning they would resume their journey once again, and Dickson anticipated a joyful reunion with the Donaldsons at Birch Cove.

They were up early on Monday morning, 6 January, and hurried to the depot to catch the first train for Halifax. The railroad between Windsor and Halifax was the first in Nova Scotia, having opened just three years earlier. Dickson and Hernandez purchased their tickets for the stop at Four Mile House, an inn four miles outside of Halifax. Dickson was anxious to get to his uncle's home at "Birch Cove," which was located about six miles northwest of Halifax.[10] When the

The old Windsor Bridge over the river Avon as it would have appeared to Dickson and Hernandez. This bridge was built in 1836 and was used until it caught fire in 1887 and collapsed into the river. The bridge to the rear was the railroad crossing. Courtesy of the Nova Scotia Archives and Records Management.

train's departure was announced, Dickson and Hernandez grabbed their baggage and boarded. Dickson wrote,

> On Monday morning we left Windsor and friends behind us as the cars start out of the station. Deep snow on each side of us. The deep dark green of the hemlocks and spruce trees relieve in beautiful contrast the dazzling white of the now sparkling snow, the sun throwing his golden rays on this network of frost with the brilliancy of midsummer. All is one continuous scene of unsurpassed loveliness, skirting some lake or through forests, over ravines or across hills all the same ever varying, always beautiful scenes. The guard, on entering the car, recognizes me at once and promises that "Everything shall be all right at 4-Mile-house."

After about an hour's train ride, Dickson and Hernandez arrived at Four Mile House in Rockingham, four miles north of Halifax. Dickson continued his diary narrative: "We bundle out with our baggage at old Davey's, placing John the hostler in charge [of the baggage] until called for. How we hurry on over the crispen snow, our voices ring out on the pure exhilarant air, and from quickening our step we soon run a race. How buoyant are our spirits. How completely have we forgot our past difficulties."

Dickson and Hernandez shuffled through the snow along the roadside, leaving the Four Mile House behind them as they plodded northward, toward Birch Cove. The road ran along the base of a rocky, snow-covered ridge that gradually sloped upward on the west side of the road while the waters of Bedford Basin spread out to the east. The railroad tracks threaded their way along the narrow shoulder of land between the road and Bedford Basin. A mile or so above Four Mile House, the west shore of Bedford Basin makes a gentle curve to create a cove about a mile across, named Birch Cove. From the south end of the cove Dickson and Hernandez could see the gables of the Donaldson home in the distance, among the trees on the slope of the ridge behind the cove. In a short time they were on the doorstep of the large house. Dickson wrote, "A surprise to 'the good folks' was my arrival at the Cove. A happy greeting and a hearty welcome I was received with." Dickson and Hernandez had arrived at the house of his aunt and uncle, Peter and Susannah Donaldson, and their children, Jane,

Katherine, Peter, Sarah Ann, Susan, Helen, Emma, and Thomas. With the aura of the holidays still in evidence, Dickson and Hernandez merely brought with them another reason to celebrate.[11]

During the next six weeks, Dickson set his diary aside while he and Hernandez enjoyed something of a winter vacation with the Donaldsons. There was much to appreciate in Halifax and many good people to keep them company. The city was still in the grip of many ongoing holiday celebrations, and a variety of military units were in town in response to preparations for the possibility of war between the United States and Great Britain over the *Trent* affair. The unauthorized seizure of Mason and Slidell, two Confederate commissioners, from the British mail packet *Trent* caused an international crisis until the Lincoln government yielded to British pressure and released the two men.

Dickson wrote about their stay in Halifax during this period of time:

"Halifax" was enjoying itself. The Sleighing Carnival was at its height and although Merry Old Christmas had come and gone again yet he had left all his fun and cheer as well as his evergreen wreaths and boughs of holly behind him. Halifax streets were enlivened with the bands of the now fast arriving regiments, brilliant with the dashing uniforms of the Guards, Rifles, Artillery etc. of the British Army. Squads of men-of-war sailors at every turn were to be met with. The gay shop windows still reminded you of Holiday presents. All seemed happy, everything gay and busy, even the harbor was filled with shipping from fishing schooners to the splendid "Canarder" and stately ships of war.

Some six weeks continued [this] round of pleasure, shooting, sleighing and parties, soon passed over. Frolics up to the French Village, up to Sackville bridge on the "What do you say for a ride to Dutch Town after tea?" What preparations, getting the box sled ready for a good old fashioned frolic, packing it with clean straw from the barn. How impatient the very horses are to be off as we tumble the girls in.[12] How happy all, how full of joy each heart as we glide like the wind itself over the pure and frozen snow for 15 miles. Another tumbling and jumping out at Mrs. Hornes and because the girls kiss Harriet we must all do the same. The dancing and fiddling and singing, and feasting and then the coming home at 2 o'clock in the morning. The fiddle and sleigh-bells chiming in

Aerial view of modern-day Halifax. Bedford Basin, with Birch Cove, is seen at the distant upper right. Courtesy of the Nova Scotia Communication and Information Centre.

The Four Mile House, where Dickson and Hernandez got off the train for the short walk to Birch Cove. This view was taken in the late nineteenth century during an American-Canadian boating competition, but it would have looked much the same to James and Tom. Courtesy of the Nova Scotia Archives and Records Management.

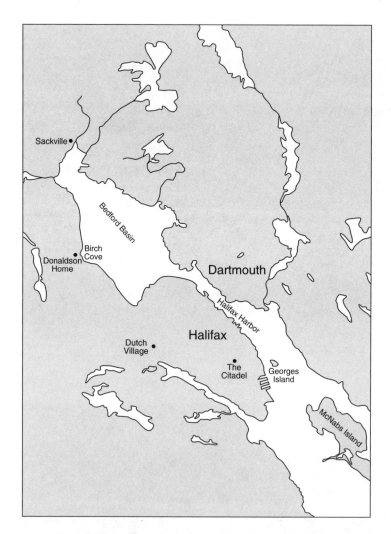

sweet melody to the musical voices singing the very appropriate air of "Old Folks at Home" and the merry musical laugh ringing out in the clear cold air, and the snowballing taken and given all in good cheer.

And so, for a few weeks, Dickson and Hernandez could forget about the war, their storm-tossed passage up the northeast coast, and the reason they had come to Halifax. Family, friends, and fun times demanded their attention during this interlude, but the time for their return would come soon enough.

⊷⊜ THREE ⊜⊶

Bound for Georgia

anuary gave way to February, and the time soon came for James Dickson and Tom Hernandez to renew their journey to Georgia. For six weeks they had enjoyed a winter vacation among the Donaldsons and friends near Halifax, but the date of their departure soon came even though the weather was not very cooperative. Dickson recorded in his diary: "Even these jolly times had an end and ere the time was up we had completed our arrangements for leaving the hospitable shores of Nova Scotia and again embarking on the treacherous ocean. Wednesday night 19th [of] February all ready for sea, but the heaviest snow storm of the season set in."

On 20 February the two men tried to get to their ship, but the weather prevented their departure. Dickson recorded, "Snowing heavy, but [we] packed into the sleigh and attempted to get into town but could not reach even 'Black Dog Hill' this snow was so deep. We soon went up [to] the gates [of the farm] knowing full well the brig would not go out that day. Today was spent pleasantly, but yet the thought of parting perhaps on the morrow saddens our pleasure yet we were still amongst kind, good friends and were therefore almost happy."

The following morning, 21 February, they found the weather more suitable for their departure. Dickson noted, "Weather clear, wind from the northwest. Early breakfast. At nine [o'clock A.M.] we bid goodby to the Cove. Leaving amidst many regrets and well wishes the very warm friends behind us, as we set out on the long journey before us

Halifax harbor as seen from the Citadel in the late nineteenth century, appearing much as it would have to Hernandez and Dickson. The community of Dartmouth is seen across the harbor. Courtesy of the Nova Scotia Archives and Records Management.

not knowing when we shall return. . . . Dispatching a few lines to my dear Mother and to the Cove I bid Uncle Peter goodbye."

Dickson's uncle William Donaldson and his cousin Tom Donaldson prepared the horse-drawn sleigh to take them to Halifax. The bags were loaded, and after saying farewell to family and friends at Birch Cove, the group climbed into the sleigh and departed. They proceeded down the snowy road that wound along the shore of Birch Cove and Bedford Basin bound for Halifax. The weather was brisk, and snow covered everything, but the snow had ceased to fall, and the road was cleared enough to enable them to pick their way through the drifts. They retraced their steps of six weeks before, following the road south, past the Four Mile House and on toward the city. Dickson recorded, "Our old friend Primy [the horse] has a hard job of it dragging us through the drifts. Even Uncle [William] has failed to appear cheerful; but by way of stimulating us as well as himself, surmised that [it] being Friday no sailor would go to sea and thinks it is not probable she will sail before Monday and then we will have another frolic; but fate has decreed it otherwise."

Dickson and Hernandez had arranged to sail aboard the brigantine *Standard*, owned by Daniel Huntley and built in Cornwallis in 1855. Windsor, Nova Scotia, was registered as its homeport, and a Captain Blanch commanded.[1] They were soon at the dockside where they found the *Standard* tied up. Its masts and rigging glittered with ice, and icicles hung from all the exposed upper works. The bay was clogged with chunks of ice, and the sky was overcast with clouds of mottled hues of gray. The hills across the bay were pure white with snow, and here and there patches of evergreen could be seen. Directly across the bay a smudge of buildings showed where the community of Dartmouth lay.

When Dickson and Hernandez arrived on board, they found at least one familiar face, that of William Crowell, the first mate from the *Lilly Dale* who had accompanied them on their storm-tossed voyage from New York. Dickson recorded their departure in his diary:

> Uncle William and cousin Tom and three or four others are at the end of the wharf. They alone are aware of our departure. Another shake hands and we are hoisting our single reef top sail from the pier.
>
> Once more afloat and this time on the brigantine "Standard" of Windsor, N.S., ten [men] all told on board, drawing 9 feet, tonnage 110. Assorted cargo of groceries, medicines, boots, dry goods, lead and gun caps and cleared for Metamoras, Mexico. However, as none expect to see nor wish to see [Mexico] at least this voyage it is very reasonable to suppose we are to run the blockade on the Georgia coast unless wrecked or captured.
>
> As we run rapidly out [of] the harbor, the water of the deepest blue is dotted with white canvas of inward and outward bound crafts amongst which is a noble looking steamer, a government steam transport from England with a large number of the Royal Artillery, bound in. Dartmouth is a very pretty town across the harbor lying at the foot of the high ridge of forest covered hills. It was the scene of many thrilling and dreadful deeds during the earlier settlement of Nova Scotia. Further on is the noble building set apart by the Provincial government for the insane.
>
> The city rises above the masts of its shipping and stretches away up and around "the hill" until the Citadel with its bastions crowns the summit, its guns pointing in every conceivable angle.

This fortification is undoubtedly one of the finest pieces of engineering work on this Continent.

George's Island with its water batteries, forts and redoubts is passed and amidst a tolerable amount of confusion of getting all to rights. Setting the watches we are fast leaving Halifax astern, gradually blending with the horizon and concealed until a single spire and the lofty chimney at Richmond Station alone mark its site. Stiff breeze blowing from the nor-west and the temperature cold. Sky clear with favorable indications of good weather.

The *Standard* proceeded out onto the open seas. Once the sails were all set and the vessel was in good order, there was time to relax. Dickson wrote, "At 4:00 P.M. 'Sambro Light' bore nor-west distance 10 miles. Had a social drink in our little cabin wishing success to our voyage and a speedy return to Nova Scotia's shores. We were fast losing sight of the coast and as the sun went down we were alone as we all had often been before on [the] broad Atlantic."

The morning of 22 February found Dickson and Hernandez forging ahead aboard the *Standard* en route to the Georgia coast. However, the crew was somewhat indisposed from the "social drink" of the night

Aerial view of the Citadel overlooking Halifax harbor. Courtesy of the Nova Scotia Archives and Records Management.

The entrance to Halifax harbor as seen from the Citadel in the late nineteenth century, a few decades after Dickson and Hernandez had departed aboard the Standard. *Georges Island is seen to far left. Courtesy of the Nova Scotia Archives and Records Management.*

before. Dickson noted, "Saturday morning the wind had failed us but we had logged during the whole night 10 knots. We were now actually in another climate. The snow and ice we had in our rigging when leaving port was now fast disappearing. We have a first rate cook and plenty of everything on board and anticipate making a quick run <u>Somewhere</u>. Our crew are just the lads, all good sailors but are a little the worse off for too much '<u>rum</u>.' However today [it] is 'tapering off' and by Sunday they will be in as good [a] trim as the '<u>Standard</u>.' Their physique [*sic*] was splendid and a daring that bespoke them as the fellows in the time of need."

On 23 February, the weather became increasingly rough, and they noticed that the ship's barometer had begun to drop, which foretold the coming of more heavy weather. The following day, 24 February, the rolling seas caused some cargo to break loose from its lashings, but the crew quickly resecured it. With a gale imminent Dickson had little time for writing in his journal, and he managed only a few lines that day. The entry reads: "Monday—Some seal [oil barrels] rolling [about]. Secured our traps from breaking loose and rolling about. Not much cooked in the galley today. Barometer still falling."

Bound for Georgia

A view of Halifax as seen from Georges Island in the harbor. The Citadel appears atop the hill at left center. Courtesy of the Nova Scotia Archives and Records Management.

By 25 February they had their hands full, as the weather continued to deteriorate. Dickson wrote,

> Kept gradually shortening sail. Barometer still falling. The mercury had gone down so low we looked for a leak but it was no leak and as we were now in the gulf there could be no doubt we were going to [have] a pretty heavy blow and we would no doubt get enough of it. Thermometer near my bunk marks 70 deg[rees] farrenheit [*sic*]. —Wind to the south'ard and east'ard heading south by west, up to noon. Headed afterwards sou-west by south. Took in top gallant sail and reefed the topsail. Sent down the top-gallant and top-mast stay sail and stowed the top-sail.
>
> About 4:00 P.M.—Sea rapidly rising and wind still increasing. Stowed the main sail, shortly after the main-stay sail blown all to ribbons. Set the storm tri-sail and hove to. [It is] now blowing fearful. The brig as yet is making good weather of it, but during the entire night the gale is increasing. All are anxious and as we have done everything, it now depends upon the <u>Brig</u> to do her duty. One squall after another succeeds with fearful rapidity accompanied with rain and hail, thunder and lightning.

The gales continued unabated during the night of 25 February and into the morning of 26 February. Those aboard the *Standard* spent the night being tossed about on the raging sea while wind and rain buffeted the ship constantly. The arrival of morning showed no signs that the storm had any intention of letting up. In fact, it looked to be getting steadily worse. Dickson recorded in his diary on the twenty-sixth:

About daylight, "All hands on deck" to secure the storm-tri-sail blown clean from the hooks. Took sea over the quarter drenching things pretty generally, even to our little cabin. The force of the wind was so great in this last squall that the iron hook in the tack that secured the bonnet of the tri-sail, although an inch and a half thick, was pulled out as straight as a poker. . . .

No fire in the galley today, that is very evident. Shipped another sea over the bulwarks, [that] stove in the galley doors. Water cask got adrift and considerable trouble in securing it. After securing the galley doors and planking, Ben called all hands below in the cabin as the forecastle was untenable. Had some hardtack and raw ham served out and water. Our crew were cold, wet and hungry, but even amongst these trials the joke would pass around [and] the Captain gave us all hands a good pull out of his own demi-john to keep up all our spirits. He, poor fellow, was lying in his bunk sick.

It was evident that the brig was either not making as good weather of it or the seas were still rising. Ben had just come below from securing his things in the galley and was about going up the Companion Way to take the man at the wheel his grog when we heard him sing out. In a moment she rolled heavily down to windward. Our cabin became dark as midnight and a fearful sea broke right upon us. Thank God all were below but the man lashed to the wheel. Our sky light was dashed in and torrents of water came down upon us, in bunks, amongst clothes, bread, saturating everything.

Our brig had been completely swept, all our lee bulwarks gone, [life]boat stove to atoms, galley torn up from the deck and swept overboard with stove, coppers, barrel beef and pork, torn from the lashings on deck, chain cable all adrift, water washing down hatchways, forecastle and cabin swimming. In an instant [Captain] Blanch was on deck, in his drawers and shirt and as he roared out "Secure the pieces of the boat my Bullies" took the wheel and sent the nearly drowned man down for coils of rope. I never will forget [Charley] the 2nd Mate's answer to the poor cook who was lamenting the loss of his pots and pans. "<u>Hold your tongue, never mind the galley, God knows but the next sea may be our last</u>."

The sea was now washing our decks from forward, clean up to the half deck. Every once in a while one of those dark masses of water would come thundering down on us seemingly to sweep us again, yet a slight motion of the wheel and it would rush like a giant past our stern, giving us a left hander that would shake every timber in her; and as we rolled into the trough of the sea, one of these dark, massive, angry waves bound our horizon as if ready to complete the work of destruction on our little brig that others had begun. But the good God alone has the ruling of the ocean. May He take us in His keeping and yet bring us in safety to port.

About 5 P.M.—Raw ham and hardtack and water. The only bread [we have] is two barrels, one of which is damaged. No other cooked victuals on board and no means of cooking, with the prospect of laying to and drifting to [the] eastward for some days. We had to set our wits to work. We had plenty of flour in the half-deck and plenty of fish, also butter, in the cargo. We all wished ourselves again in sight of Sambro [Light] that we might refit.

It is very evident when this gale abates we must make for some port to repair damages. Halifax, Bermuda and even Nassau, each have been recommended as being advantageous; but that will depend upon the wind and our position when the gale ceases. However, the sooner we are all in port, the better, for all hands are starving, or next door to it. Is not just exactly what readers of miraculous escapes at sea [might] imagine it to be. . . .

Occasionally we get a little salt water over us, but thank God during the night we manage to escape any of the seas [from] boarding [us]. At times the rolling of the brig amongst the mountain[ous] seas will throw you in a most violent manner from one side of your bunk to the other and requires some skill to prevent being thrown out altogether; and if you are on your feet, the utmost care and exertion is necessary to prevent your being dashed in a most unceremonious and undignified manner from leeward to windward and back by way of rather a rough admonition of "Look out for yourself next time, Sir." A few accidents occurred such as bruised shins and cracked heads but fortunately none were of a serious nature.

The morning of 27 February found the situation unchanged aboard the *Standard* as the crew continued to struggle through a winter gale that seemed intent on tearing the vessel apart. It was certainly no pleasure cruise, as Dickson recorded in his diary:

Thursday morning 27th: Two hard biscuits, a piece or rather hunk, of raw ham and [a] drink of water. Everything wet and disagreeable on board but the steward draws all our attention from wet clothes and bunks to the fact that there is only one ham left. We do not think the raw ham so bad after all, and again the matter is vividly brought before us that things cannot last long this way. Our biscuits, i.e. hardtack, is getting less and less every meal and [we are] still laying to, driving further and further to the eastward and the gale blowing as fierce as ever from the west, nor'west and a rather slim prospect of running to westward for some days yet. Our decks are always covered with water and frequently over the tops of our hatches.

8 Bells—Noon: Hardtack and butter dealt out. How a cup of good coffee would be appreciated now, or how would we relish a drink of milk from the Cove. However, the gale makes us more anxious than even our grub.

The storm continued unabated as the vessel plowed ahead through the high seas, rain, and winds. The crewmen clung to the ship and fought to keep it afloat for it was their only hope of survival. There was little else they could do, but for all the anguish and excitement of the storm, there was also an element of frustration and boredom as they had little to occupy their time during the evenings except each other's company. On the night of 27 February, Dickson recorded,

What a strange picture tonight does our little 8 by 12 box of a cabin present. The dim flickering light from our lantern shedding its dull, lurid light upon us from the stanchion above and all of us huddled together only excepting the man at the wheel on deck. Some perched in bunks, on chests, or a few even amidst the water slushing back and forward on the cabin floor, encased in oil skin and sou'westers, all munching and forcing down the hardtack.

The cook and John Day declare their intentions to rig out a new gear for the stove pipe to prevent the gale [from] blowing out the fire from the stove as it has done on every attempt to light the little coffee-pot-looking stove in our cabin. Ben shows with much glee an old tea-pot. This creates so much satisfaction that [Captain] Blanch give us a good pull out of his demi-john of Jamaica [rum]. Of course the drink and the tea-pot together could not fail to raise our spirits. Then came the not overly polite inquiries in reference to certain lost, as well as stolen, plugs of <u>Negro Head</u> [tobacco].

Charley the 2nd Mate, a huge looking specimen of Salt Water Fraternity from New Foundland, his feet hid by a pair of huge cow skin boots, his body enveloped in oil clothes, a long white night cap surmounts his head. A tassel of rope yarns hangs from and falls on the side, resting on a most piratical looking beard, as he braces himself up to meet the sudden roll of the brig. His head enveloped with a blue cloud of smoke from an outrageous pipe filled with a most vile quality of Pig Tail, [he] asks with a knowing look "Well boys, who the H—wouldn't sell a farm and go to Sea?" Hard compliments and rough jokes that would give a Frenchman the Staggers are given and received until the man at the wheel is relieved and we turn in to pass another not altogether comfortless night thanking God it is no worse.

The gale was still tossing the vessel about on 28 February, but it now looked as if it might weather the blow after all. The day was not without some small successes. Dickson recorded additional observations in his diary:

After many failures [we] at last succeeded in getting our cockle shell stove lit and were soon boiling our salt-herring and potatoes, frying salt pork and wound up by brewing our tea. Of course all this took time but we did not waste precious moments by overcooking. Our teapot is a great institution when the gale allows us to use it. It cooks and boils and brews all we eat and drink.

Our spirits are like the weather glass. In fact rises and falls with it. At times all are desponding again [but] with the slightest evidence of a change for the better all is fun to drive dull care away.

There is no doubt but this has been one of the most violent gales that anyone on board has witnessed. Many surmises are made regarding the vessels in our vicinity, particularly of an American Bark bound on our course and apparently in the South American trade.

The *Standard* remained in the grips of an unrelenting North Atlantic gale that buffeted the vessel unmercifully. It was all the crew could do to ride it out in their tiny cabin and take turns topside at the wheel. For several days the storm prevented Dickson from making any entries in his diary; however, on 5 March he managed to record a single, brief entry since it was his twenty-sixth birthday. He wrote, "My birthday, but only a repetition of Christmas and New Years discomforts and dangers."

By 7 March the winter gale that had tossed them about for two weeks finally began breaking up. In fact, they were able to get the ship under sail once again, even though the wind was still gusting badly. Dickson recorded a short entry in his diary on this day. "This is our fifteenth day out. Wind still heavy from the nor'west. Bore up for Bermuda, as we had been lying to up to this morning. We got the brig about and steered for Bermuda." It seemed as though their situation was finally beginning to change for the better.

The storm gradually subsided, and by 9 March the *Standard* found the weather situation decidedly improved. Now that the gale at last was breaking up, they began figuring out how far off course they had been blown. A check of their charts and navigational readings showed that the storms had blown them off course far to the east of Bermuda. But with good weather they hoped to make up for lost time. Dickson took a moment to record in his diary: "We are by dead reckoning 112 miles east of the island [of Bermuda] . . . and nearly a thousand miles to the eastward of our true course."

By 11 March, the *Standard* was finally on course again with the blessing of clear weather, but in contrast to the storms of weeks past, the morning found them becalmed, with clear skies and no wind to fill their sails. Dickson and his companions used the slack time for some recreation and to make repairs to the vessel. Dickson finally had time to return to his diary and record a long entry after several days of almost total silence.

A dead calm, our sails flapping against the masts with every roll of the vessel. Immense fields of Gulf weed floating slowly past us. The silvery flying fish springing from the sea and seeking a temporary refuge in its short lived flight over the tops of the waves, from its voracious and unrelenting foe, the Dolphin.

Sharks are around us in dozens. One old man eater of these waters got a couple of doses in the shape of buck-shot from my double barrel gun. His flight was so rapid that we could hardly follow him with the eye. In an instant a drove of the voracious monsters were after their wounded mate. We hooked another but unfortunately he was too strong or our line too weak and [we] lost him, as well as the pork [used as bait]. We hooked several but they all got away from us. Of course the hatred of these monsters of the deep were the maledictions of all hands, heaped upon the offender who would seize our piece of pork and make good his escape.

As we're running to the southward now it was likely we would have good weather. Our hardtack nearly all gone. We built a fire on the chain cable, forward, and set John Day to work. [He] melted down the fat pork and fried Slap Jacks on a shovel. John had seen that done on the Paradise from which he had, with a portion of her crew, been rescued in December last. They were tip-top and whatever faults they had or would have had on shore were entirely overlooked here. We were compelled also now to live on Slap Jacks altogether as today a misfortune occurred that was never dreamed of. Our tea-pot or rather the bottom had given out from real hard service.

Since the Standard's lifeboat had been severely damaged by the rough weather, it was decided to effect some sort of repair. A leaky boat was better than no lifeboat. Dickson wrote, "Nearly all hands put to work on our broken and crushed boat. [Captain] Blanch is a first rate carpenter and with the boards of our bunks managed in four or five days, had a pretty substantial boat re-built and caulked. This looked certainly like surmounting our difficulties."

On the morning of 15 March, the Standard was begining to sail into more stormy weather. During the day Dickson took time to record a lengthy entry in his diary:

Saturday morning a schooner [was seen] lying some 5 miles to eastward of us. A Dutchman's gale of wind straight up and down the Mast. [We] lowered the boat from the davits after breakfast, bailed her out, put a barrel of flour, jug of water, four men and set the coxswain [aboard]. Boat leaking pretty freely. Set off for the schooner to procure some bread and if possible a pot for our barrel of flour. They were nearly eight hours away. They reported the schooner from St. Johns, New Brunswick bound to Jamaica with deals.[2]

[They] had nearly four feet of water in [their] hold. At the pumps nearly all the time. Had left a week later than we and had consequently not been in the severest of the gale. They had been on the point of abandoning her but had lost boats and had seen no vessels since leaving the Bay. Had lost their provisions such as bread and flour consequently our barrel was quite acceptable. They offered us beef or pork in return but as we had plenty did not accept. They sent us 20 lbs cooked rye, a pillow case of oatmeal and a cracked pot to answer as a stove. Requested them to report us 23 days out bound to Metamoros, Mexico. We were, according to the schooner's log, by dead reckoning in Longitude 57-degrees, which if proved to be correct would place us further to the eastward than we had calculated or even dreamed.

As the wind was springing up and rapidly freshening, the Standard was headed west by south. We were now leaving the schooner fast astern and as night closed in on us we lost sight of our New Brunswick friend. During the absence of our boat light puffs of wind followed by a steady breeze caused us to back the top-sails to prevent us [from] shooting ahead. In the last two hours everything had altered materially. Our boat on deck and well lashed, keel up, on the main hatch and the Royal and gaf-top sail furled. At 4 Bells we felt as if we had been fortunate in having completed our duty and just as the cook is coming aft with our mess of "Slap Jacks."

4 Bells—"Supper forward and aft" roars out the cook. Another interesting group on board the Standard. All of us on the windward side of the Quarter Deck huddled around our dish of Slap Jacks [and] pint tin mug half full of molasses from which all dip in the most thoroughly democratic manner imaginable. All idle forms and silly etiquet are abolished by even those more refined. Jokes pass

quickly around our situation, [which] gives rise to many a laugh. Even our hardships and dangers are forgot in the desire to appease our hunger. Ben the cook, not to be behind his now rival, John Day of Shovel notoriety, has brewed us tea in the fluid can.[3] This raises the old mates spirits a degree at least, higher and he cracks to our side of the mess a man-of-wars yarn whilst John Day and the Cook are carrying on a lively discussion in reference to the capabilities of each other in cooking on board of vessels in situations similar to our own. Occasionally the spray comes over the quarter as the Standard now rushed like a race horse at the rate of 8 knots by the log. The mug of Tea takes the place of the punch bowl and we drink it to the Captain's "Saturday night sweethearts and wives." Each thinks of home and the dear ones far away o'er the main.

The approach of a gale of wind on the ocean is frequently attended with signs and portents as sublime as any fancy can conceive. The sky to the eastward was heavy, dark and foreboding. From the horizon was fast rising, angry masses of clouds. The sea rose and fell sullenly, black as night. Away astern as we flew on like the wind, we left a long white line of foam as straight as an arrow that marked our course over this mighty world of waters. In the west the sky was spread with the gold and crimson fires, the most gorgeous sunset I ever beheld. The sun partly hid in a bank of clouds that reflected a thousand shades of color on either side, reaching down to the horizon where long pale yellow streaks of light which had burst through the less dense folds of vapor forming what Sailors technically termed "wind galls" were almost straight up in the heavens.

[With] the creaking of the spars from the increased pressure of the wind upon the canvas, the wind whistled shrilly through the rigging, or sighed mournfully as it swept through the blocks as if singing a requiem over many a lost mariner entombed beneath the treacherous waves. This evening when the Sun again sank beneath the sea it was indeed a sight of splendor and magnificence and as the strange sounds of warning fell upon our ears breaking the silence of the scene, it rendered a sight almost supernatural and even one of terror. The voice of [Captain] Blanch on the rising gale arouses all. "Reef-top-sail, take in top gallant sail, send down the top-mast-stay-sail." All were aware that "dirty weather" is in store for us, however this time the gale was from the right direction. The plunging of the brig, the roaring of the increasing gale, lulled us into sleep as we turned in to our bunks once more to rest.

On 16 March, the *Standard* was well into another heavy gale; however, it was blowing the ship in the right direction for a change. Dickson recorded some of the day's events in his diary.

Blowing very heavy. [We] are reduced to a close reefed topsail and fore stay-sail and the prospects [are] of not being able to carry that very long. We are now driving dead before it at a fearful rate. Scudding is the most dangerous mode of sailing and is only done when the danger is eminent. It is always a trying time on board of any ship.

We are driving with both sea and wind [behind us]. The huge seas rushing after and rolling past us in their expended strength [and] again rising as we [are] swept by, threatening to overtake and engulf us. At times in these trying moments [she] would roll onwards on the crest of one of these monsters of the deep as steadily as if at anchor. At the next, when she would get for a second beyond the control of her rudder, she would roll to port almost and at times actually burying the top-gallant-sail. As she would recover the next instant, her other quarters would be so deeply and suddenly thrown against the sea, threatening to turn us bottom up altogether. As she would gradually rise up her decks would be relieved of the immense pressure upon them, the water running down the scuppers and pouring in volumes past the bulwark stanchion into the sea. Planks had been lashed and boards nailed across the stanchion to prevent such seas [from] going over our decks, our bulwarks having been carried away previously. Our feeble attempts at ship carpentry (all that our limited means would allow) were all useless. The heavy masses of water was too much for even wood and iron. They were ripped up and carried away until we had no more to replace them with.

So great a quantity of water continually sweeping over our decks caused us much uneasiness about our hatches, however they were lashed and battened down as well [as] they could be and that was as satisfactory as we could expect. [Still] water was going down our hatches in addition to the leak at the heel of the bow sprit that was pouring in a continuous stream as large as a man's arm. Our timber port hole forward was also leaking badly to add to our misfortunes. The consequence was that constant attention to the pumps was requisite to keep the leak under control and the brig afloat.

No cooking today. Two cold slap jacks to each [man] and a pint of water to every two. The captain informs us all that having had one of the water casks stove [in] unfortunately, our stock is suddenly diminished to a quantity under [the] circumstances, alarmingly small. Here after the water will be under lock and key and only opened when drawn by himself and as necessary to our preservation. We would be compelled to go on allowance of one half pint a day. All would fare alike, not a drop more and if things look no better and we saw no vessels we would have to do with less. At noon the captain filled a demijohn and placed it in his bunk with strict injunctions that even should it be stole we would all hands go without for two days, so all hands were cautioned, and particularly the cook, to keep their "weather-eye" open, and keep all rogues from the water jug.

This night proved one of the most frightful of the voyage. One squall after another passed over us with fearful rapidity. Rain and hail with loud peals of thunder and the most livid flashes [of] lightning accompanied the most furious squalls. The wind was now hauling more round to the westward consequently in the puffs which strained every rope and threatened to carry away every spar as well as the canvas we were compelled to run more off our course.

At midnight all hands roused up, [it] blowing a perfect hurricane, to lay [the] ship to. We were afraid of our topmast going and the ship broaching to, which if it occurred the sea would sweep everything and the second [sea] if the first sea did not accomplish [it] would <u>finish us</u>. An anxious time. At a fitting moment helm "<u>down hard down</u>." Storm Tri-Sail rigged out, Top-Sail furled, also the Fore Top Mast Stay Sail. As our head came up to the wind and sea we felt more comfortable not withstanding the tremendous rolling that now took place. Chests, seats, everything moveable, joined the uproar in the steward's pantry. Every precaution was taken to prevent her bows [from] being knocked off by the seas and their boarding us. First Mate at the wheel.

The following morning, 17 March, found the crew still dealing with less than ideal weather. However, now that they were in a warmer climate, the storm did not have the penetrating chill of those they had come through after leaving New York City and Halifax. But the warmer climate brought new problems for the crew. Dickson recorded the day's difficulties in his diary.

The sea presents a truly grand and terrific yet sublime appearance. What more appalling sight in the entire universe than an angry raging sea. All admire, wonder and fear it. The most callous heart seeks a silent commission with its maker and sees in its fury the hand of "Omnipotence." Once or twice heavy bodies of water come pouring like a cataract over our bows striking on our decks with a dull leaden sound like sods falling on a coffin, sending a thrill to every nerve.

One of these [waves] that came on board this morning crushed the heavy planking and dashed in the forward bulwark, tore chains from the lashings and swept them aft to the half-decks, [and] carried away [the] figure head, drenching everything below in the cabin pretty thoroughly as usual. [It] stove [in] as we found out afterwards, two puncheons of seal oil in the hold. When the pumps were manned a great quantity of oil came up on deck and ran through the scuppers. I now for the first time saw the wonderful effect that oil had upon the sea. The result was indeed as extraordinary as it was instantaneous in quieting the sea in our immediate vicinity. As it ran into the sea it spread around the ship extending in a mirror-like surface to windward as well as leeward. Not a single crest of a breaking or surging sea was to be seen within its boundaries (but rose with an easy roll like a sea filled with crushed ice) whilst all about us out side of this temporary girdle of protection the sea raged with unabated fury.

Saw a vessel some five miles to windward of us. She remained in sight but a short time. She was doubtless some West Indiaman and it is to be hoped we are or will soon be even on the track of these vessels. We see immense quantities of sea weed or rather Gulf weed, driving before the gale in long narrow streaks stretching from one wave to another as far as the eye can reach in every direction. It has been driven out of the gulf by the long continuance of westerly gales.

Our small allowance of water and miserable fare added to our awful weather does not make us too cheerful by any means. So far we have bore up nobly against all our misfortunes and will endeavor, God willing, to do so to the end.

At 10 P.M. the man at the wheel reported a ball of fire on the Top-Gallant yard. It was like the flame of a large lamp of a pale yellow. It ran out and back upon the yard several times, ran down the mast to the foreyard arm, [and] ran out on the yard as if directed by a Supernatural being, and then disappeared as suddenly as it came. Of course after that there [were] curious things going to happen. Each [man] knew what was going to occur, all smacking very strongly of salt water superstitions to which I must say I was not altogether proof against. The Captain accounted [it] as a warning that the gale was nearly at its height. The nearer the deck the sooner it will be over, the higher up towards the truck, the farther off is the breaking of the gale. These meteors are called <u>St. Enoch's</u> [<u>Elmo's</u>] <u>Fire</u> and are amongst the most curious things in nature.

As we turn in leaving the man lashed to the wheel on deck, everything wet and cold below. The men are endeavoring to make the little stove burn to dry themselves by its fire, however we turn in to fight the vermin, hungry, half-famished with cold, and half starved for want of a good meal. Tom and myself had up to within a week slept in the same bunk but the vermin were rapidly increasing as we got down in this Latitude. [They] swarmed from every seam in the ship and our bunk seemed to be the Rendezvous before they started on their foraging expeditions. Everything that Lyons the Bedbug exterminator ever saw, heard, or dreamed of, tortured us. Bedbugs like snapping turtles, "grey-backs" that would almost walk away with you, shirt and all, fleas running and jumping the Zouave drill in battalions over us, cockroaches in squadrons charging to the right and left with a noise almost equal to the tramp of cavalry. Their name was legion and they were as savage as if they all had the hydrophobia. We, under the existing state of affairs, agreed to take [Captain] Blanch's and Dugan's chests, filling up the space with them under the sky light which formed a little inner cabin between our bunks. [We] spread our mattress on the chests and as the space would be pretty well filled up with Tom, Dugan, and myself, we would seek a temporary relief from the troublesome gentlemen, above [deck].

The morning of 18 March saw little change in the situation. It was another day of struggling with the elements. The contraption that Dickson, Hernandez, and Dugan had rigged up in the cabin to put them out of reach of the many insects aboard was successful for a while. However, their relief was short-lived. That night the bugs were quick to figure things out. Dickson wrote,

It was not long [that] we enjoyed our escape. The night after we vamoosed the ranche they found us out. Of course war was immediately proclaimed. We set to work burning oakum to smoke them out and nearly smothered ourselves. After scratching and killing to very little purpose we fell asleep on our wet couch [only] to be aroused in a most unceremonious and uncomfortable manner. A sea most unfortunately broke over our quarters washing the boards and canvas off and dashing in the glass of the sky light over us, in an instant deluging us with the icy cold water of the Atlantic, almost strangling us whilst thousands of fleas, bed-bugs, cockroaches, etc., etc. went into that land from which no traveler ever returns. I suppose it will always remain a question whether we or the bed-bugs were the most surprised by the unexpected cold bath.

Of course the only consolation we got was a hearty laugh from all hands at our expense. "I say skipper James," says one, as I stood holding on to a bunk, the salt water dripping from me like [a] half drowned rat, "Skipper James, I'll be damned if the sea left many bugs on you chaps." Just then we could not appreciate the joke nor the laughs cracked at our expense. We were in reality what that good old Soul Captain Truck would call "a category and be d——d to it."

On 19 March the *Standard* was still weathering the storm. The vessel handled it well, but there were other problems. Dickson noted,

Still lying to, ship making pretty fair weather of it, but a tremendous sea running, giving our stern some fearful thumps as it runs under our quarter, shaking every timber and plank in her. In fact our stern bears marks of hard usage already. Kept nearly all night the pumps going to keep the leaks under [control]. Blowing as fierce as ever but we now think the gale will break about noon or midnight.

Succeeded in getting the fire lit this morning, after many discouraging failures, in our little cockle shell stove. Ben and John Day are cooking "Slap-Jacks" under difficulties. It would make a capital scene for the comic papers or even for a painter. John Day, a colossal specimen of the "genus homo" from "Icdone" [one] of the genuine dried and salted specimens of the old Jack Tar School, holds the shovel over the stove, tilting it at every roll [of the ship] to keep both dough and grease from rolling into the fire and himself well braced forward and aft to prevent his being thrown on top of the stove to keep his Slap Jacks company.

Ben [is] well secured on the windward side of the stove pipe, half choked with soot and smoke that puffs in dense clouds through the grate [and] into the little cabin. At every roll of the ship he looks anxiously into the shovel. As soon as [the flapjack] becomes as black as the shovel [he] seizes it between his thumb and sheath knife and with a grunt of satisfaction places it on a pile of its predecessors. Occasionally their laudable and highly interesting labors are suddenly interrupted by too great a quantity of salt water spray dashing into the stove pipe which is followed by some pretty tall swearing by our cook and cook's mate of which the highest point of said accomplishment can only be known to sailors. Although [it was] a pretty serious thing, ten half famished, over-worked, thirsty men to be kept alive by this, our only means of obtaining food; yet it was hard to suppress a smile or to check a laugh as some coarse witticism is cracked at the expense of our chief cook and assistant.

All happened to be below watching with much interest the increasing plate of "Slaps" when the man at the wheel [Oliver] roared down the Companion Way "Fire in the fore castle Sir! Smoke driving up the forward Companion Way!" For a moment all were paralized with fear. All believed we wouldn't reach Dixie now. After a few moments [Captain] Blanch sprung up. "Rouse up the watch! All hands on deck! Bring lanterns forward!"

As they went below what a moment of fearful uncertainty and anxiety. I believe everyone on board made up his mind that their time had come. Slap Jacks, everything was forgot, even the dangers of the sea boarding us was momentarily forgotten. At a favorable opportunity the main hatch was taken off, but thank God, revealed no fire. Some piles of wet brooms that had been jammed in to fill up an unoccupied space under the hatch were smoking and quite warm. [We] explored as far as we could go but our search found nothing on fire. It was now quite evident, that the smoke which came down our stove pipe in puffs was driven from our cabin by the wind, down our Companion Way into the half deck and through the ship forward into the Fore Castle. So far, so good, but it was sometime before we recovered [from] the shock [of] "Fire in the forecastle sir!"

On 20 March the gale finally began to break up, allowing the crew to put the vessel back on course for the Georgia coast. Dickson only took time to record a few lines in his diary: "As was expected yesterday [that] the gale would break during the night, [the] weather much more moderate [today]. Wind and sea fast going down. About 4 P.M. put ship on her course as near as the sea would let us. Steering westsouthwest."

By the twenty-first the weather cleared completely, and the *Standard* was blessed with good sailing for a change. Dickson noted,

Running with all sail set. Fair wind for a wonder. If we can hold on for several days at this rate we will be in the Gulf [Stream] after which a few hours will decide whether we shall arrive on the coast of the Confederate States or be taken by the Yankees as a prize.

About 8 bells [Noon]: A spar was reported dead ahead standing upright in the water, we running at 9 knots to the westward. At first we supposed it to be a spar buoy that had been driven by the long continuous [line] of westerly gales, across the Gulf Stream and away out here far to the eastward, but as we came rapidly down upon it a second mast was [seen] standing abaft the first. It was now clearly a wreck.

As we passed it we ascertained it to be some unfortunate vessel. Her fore and main masts alone rose above the water. Her hull was entirely below the surface. Top masts and cross trees had been cut or carried away. They were perhaps 15 feet above the ocean. What she was or what she had been or the fate of those on board, God only knew. We supposed she was loaded with deals and had become waterlogged after being disabled.[4] We passed one or two water casks which had no doubt belonged to the unfortunate vessel. Such is often the sad end of the seaman's life. It was soon far astern, its masts still looming solitarily upwards above the wide waste of waters.

On the morning of 22 March the *Standard* was forging ahead and making good time. After the gales of weeks past, the clear, bright skies overhead were a welcome sight. But clear sailing weather did not bring an end to their difficulties. Dickson wrote,

> Wind failing, that is, not so strong as yesterday. In the morning [we] passed immense quantities of Gulf weed as [is] usual in mild weather, passing us in great fields. Caught several "Dolphin." Baited the hook with a small piece of white rag, trolling astern. They seize it eagerly, mistaking it as it passes quickly over the tops of the waves, for the beautiful and curious flying-fish.
>
> The beauty of the Dolphin has not been exaggerated. The fish when hauled up on deck is the picture of beauty and speed. The power of changing its colors when dying is wonderful and surprisingly beautiful. The most brilliant shades of gold, green, crimson, silver and blue, flashing in the sun light, fading, re-appearing and blending in the most exquisite tints of the rainbow. They are excellent eating but when boiling, a piece of silver is always placed in the pot along-side of it. At times they are poisonous and it is detected by the silver turning black when they are unsafe to eat.
>
> The ocean is alive today, schools of porpoises are sporting about the bows and we are rigging out a harpoon. Occasionally a silver like flying fish flies on board as if to seek shelter from the dolphin who pursued it with unrelenting fury and speed. Portuguese Men-of-War with their sails set pass us dancing over the waves. At times one [of] these frail barks are capsized by a puff of wind. They are amongst the most singular organizations on the Atlantic. Latitude today 26 degrees.

After several weeks of working together for their mutual survival, the crewmen of the *Standard* were by now a well-knit group. Of course, after all this time in the close proximity of one another, within the restricting confines of the ship, it was not unusual for tempers to flare. Their nerves were probably all a little frayed, and shortages of fresh water and food were only some of the problems they faced aboard ship. But the scarcity of tobacco was the one thing that was sorely felt.

However, what angered some, brought a smile to the others. Dickson wrote,

> All hands had run out of tobacco nearly a week ago, consequently many things are substituted. Coffee is smoked (ground), oakum is smoked and chewed. Tea however is more in favor for smoking as well as chewing. It is considered almost equal to tobacco.
>
> An amusing incident took place today. The 1st Mate, Hutchinson, it appears had been in the habit for a week past every day after dinner of re-chewing an <u>old cud</u> of tobacco and always after re-hiding it away in the binnacle for future use. As was found out afterwards, <u>Charley</u>, [the] 2nd Mate, had watched him and found where the coveted prize was hid. Accordingly when <u>Hutchinson</u> went below to turn in, <u>Charley</u> removed the <u>oft-chewed</u>, <u>veteran cud</u> from the binnacle to his own mouth. The following day he dried it and smoked it in his pipe. So, today Hutchinson stole slyly to the binnacle for his valued morsel. The treasure was gone. <u>Charley</u> had been seen smoking real tobacco instead of rope yarns, so the mystery was explained and a big row between the mates was the result.

On 23 March the *Standard* was closing the distance between it and the Georgia coast. The weather continued to be favorable, and the crew's attention was now focused on preparing their vessel for the eventual run through the blockade. Dickson noted,

> This morning a light breeze, but during the night it was nearly a calm. We must be approaching the warm outer bands of the Gulf [Stream]. We are caulking our port Timber Hole, mending sails and getting everything in readiness for running in or running away from the "<u>Blockaders</u>" as everything is overhauled. If we only get the wind, this entire Yankee fleet will have their hands full to catch us. Opened the hatches to dry things below. Almost everything is more or less damaged excepting the medicines which are aft under the half-deck.
>
> After our frugal but welcome breakfast [I] had my accustomed bath, the cook dashing a good dozen buckets of the clear, blue, icy water from the ocean right and left over me which I think has gone far to brace my system up to the hardships and discomforts of this protracted voyage. . . . Today [I] lost part of my water I had hid. However, some fellows allowance will have to suffer. I see it is

necessary to keep your weather eye open all the time below as well as on deck. I will be topside with someone if I have to rob the cook's pantry. . . .

This afternoon [a] dead calm, sails flapping and striking heavily against the masts. A gale of wind would be preferable to this dull monotonous inactivity. However we are of the opinion that we will have wind enough as our old friend the barometer has again fallen.

24 March was a day of good weather and freshening winds on the southeast Atlantic. The *Standard* proceeded to close in on the Georgia coast. Dickson noted, "Wind freshening from the eastward. All in high glee. All sail set, [making] 6 knots. Looking out for the warm bands [in the water] which will denote our approaching the Gulf [Stream]. Looking rather rough to the eastward. Battened down the hatches again about 3 P.M. Blowing fresh [and] furled the Royal sail."

A short time later the lookout sighted a sail some distance ahead of them. This was the first vessel they had come across in quite some time, and this indicated they were indeed getting close to the shipping lanes in the Gulf Stream. Dickson continued his narrative:

[The ship] dead ahead soon proved to be a large bark, close hauled and dashing ahead [at] 8 knots and showing Spanish colors. We were bowling off our 10 to 11 [knots and] ran up the breeze the blood-stained flag of old England. How proudly were its folds thrown to the wind as it ran up to the peak of the Standard, she rushing through the brine with the swiftness of the race horse.

[We] wished to exchange longitude with him but the Spaniard was too slow in making his figures as in a few seconds almost, they were not visible with the glass. The way it is done, [we] chalk on a large board our longitude to windward, run up the ensign, running up as near to the other ship as possible. They immediately run up their colors and show their longitude up to noon, over the stern so they may both make corrections if necessary. She was no doubt bound from Cuba to Europe.

Throughout the remainder of the day and into the night the crew of the *Standard* sought evidence that they were approaching the warmer waters of the Gulf Stream. At certain intervals a bucket of water was hauled up and its temperature checked by all hands. However, there was still no general agreement among them. Dickson wrote, "The water appeared quite warm at the next trial. As we had no thermometer detached from the barometer it was all guess work about the temperature of the water. As one [man] would pronounce a bucket of water just drawn, warm, decidedly so, a second [man] would swear it was as cold as charity."

Since they were approaching the shipping lanes in the southeast Atlantic, there were other dangers to be alert for. An inattentive lookout could prove to be the death of them all. Dickson recorded a near disaster, narrowly averted in the darkness, that almost ended their journey prematurely.

During the night [the] wind hauled around to the southward, we consequently hauled up to the northward. As the brig had been hauled up on her course about an hour, we were all roused up by the voice of the 1st [Mate]. "My God! Here is a large ship coming right down on us! Be quick! Hand up the signal lantern!" In the midst of life, we are in death. I was up on deck in an instant.

The sky was intensely dark [and] not a single star shone through the black canopy above. A flash revealed a large ship dead ahead, all sail set. It was a trying moment. We put the helm down hard. An age seemed to be passing in lighting the lantern. As it came up, the lamp fell out of the lantern. It was being in an instant relit, placed properly in the lantern and in another moment, Ben was in the weather rigging waving it. We were now so near we could hear them running about and put their helm up. In another [moment] our yards nearly touched as we passed each other. We could see the rays of light from the binnacle light shine full on the face of the man at the wheel. In another [instant] we were fast leaving each other astern. A few seconds delay in seeing her and no doubt all would have met a watery grave.

As I turned in, I felt more than ever my dependence on the Giver of all good. After that escape we kept the light lashed in the fore-weather-rigging as an ounce of prevention is worth a pound of cure. We were now right in the track of vessels from the West Indies to Europe and the Northern States, therefore, a bright light and a sharp eye to windward were necessary. Water examined several times during the night with the same unsatisfactory results.

The next day, 25 March, the *Standard* still enjoyed good, clear sailing but the crewmen were now beginning to see how far off course they had been blown by the storms. According to their calculations they should have been in the Gulf Stream off the Georgia coast, but many things told them they were still far out on the Atlantic. Dickson recorded,

> Still running west by north. [A] sharp lookout kept for the Gulf [Stream] as according to the New Brunswick Schooner's reckoning, we were into it and we thought it was impossible to be far from it. Got the "deep-sea-lead" up and coiled all ready for use on the quarter deck.[5] About noon [we] backed the top sail for sounding. All watch with intense interest, the rushing down of the line into the brine until it ran all out but without finding bottom. Water at times appears cold, at others warmer.
>
> By sunset, according to our New Brunswick friend, we would have been high and dry on the mainland. It is now evident we were driven much further to the eastward than we had or even the Schooner had calculated, and how far we were yet ignorant as we had not yet even reached the Gulf [Stream] although we had, according to the firm conviction of all on board, passed through warm and cold bands innumerable. It was now evident we were fast approaching it.
>
> The night was squally, much lightning all along the horizon to the westward. Air warm and oppressive, yet still onward we go. We can now realize the great distance we were driven off the coast. It would not have taken much more westerly wind to have driven us on the coast of Africa.

That night the ship ran into heavy weather again; however, this gale was not as severe as what the crew had endured in weeks past. The rain was now especially welcome as their stores of fresh water aboard ship were dangerously low, and efforts were made to collect as much rain-water as possible while the storm blew. But, regardless of the storm, they finally found themselves in the long-sought Gulf Stream. Dickson wrote,

> Ship lying to in the Gulf [Stream]. Blowing tremendously and an awful sea running. All hands called up to catch water [as it was] raining and hailing. [We] made a canvas trough at the foot of the

<u>Close-reefed Main-Sail</u> but [the] brig rolled so heavily [we] lose the best part of it before it is secured. All hands to leeward of the sheet with pans, buckets, and bowls catching the precious drops as they ran down from the reefing points. A good deal that was saved was only fit for cooking as it would produce a nausea to drink, being too salty. The reason was the sail was filled with salt from the spray that fell upon it. . . . [The] rain did not last, only in showers. The water we secured was nearly three buckets but it was hardly fit to drink, causing a parching thirst as well as sickness at the stomach. It does tolerable well though, to mix with our regular allowance at the rate of one third. . . .

We were driving up [to] now with the current to the northward on the southern edge of the [Gulf] stream. The gale blowing from the westward was again carrying us as well to the eastward. About 9 A.M. [wind] carried away the main-Stay sail, blown all to ribbons. . . .

Our coal and wood have given out and if we are again driven out [onto the open Atlantic] God only [knows] what will become of us. In fact we are so driven, so reduced, so completely knocked-up with our continued privations, that the main object of all on board is now to get succor and relief if we even have to ask it from our enemies. Our disabled and forlorn condition would certainly compel them to alleviate our distress, banish their suspicions as to the real motive of our voyage, and our papers would compel them to allow us to depart after supplying our wants. Our determinations were the result of despair. All fear of capture were banished as starvation and thirst were staring us straight in the face. All were reduced by the labor and hardships of the voyage.

At night we would seek our comfortless and frequently wet beds hungry, our throats, nearly parched for want of water, this night in particular, from drinking the saline water that we caught from the Main Sail during the rain squall. I thought my throat would burst [for] I was in a perfect fever. I went to [Captain] Blanch's bunk [and] begged him for some water. "Certainly Dickson," said he "here, take my share." That I have not nor shall I ever forget that generous act of that honest, true, sterling, generous-hearted British sailor. I wish him a long and pleasant journey through this life and a happy one hereafter. Yes, many a true heart beats beneath a blue jacket.

The gale began breaking up on the morning of 27 March, and with clearing weather the crew took extraordinary measures to cook their "slap jacks." Since they were out of firewood, spare spars and planks provided fuel, and an anchor chain coiled up on the deck served as the foundation on which they built their cooking fire. Dickson wrote,

This morning the wind was lulling, the gale evidently abating. The wind had veered and was coming around. We had been driven off the edge of the [Gulf] Stream during the night. About noon [we] got [the] ship again on her course. At 12 [noon] got an observation, Latitude 30 miles south of Fernandina, Florida.

[We] rigged out a piece of old sail forward to shelter our fire on the chains from being put out by the spray. Burning a spare spar. John, and Ben [are] alternately mixing and cooking dough upon our old friend the shovel. All hands aft this afternoon on the quarter deck repairing and patching the Main Stay-Sail, sky clear, weather fine. Wind southeast but a nasty sea on from the westward. [We] are consequently under reduced canvas, not daring to carry sail for fear [of] running her under altogether.

On 28 March the men of the *Standard* battled another line of storms that kept things in an unsettled state aboard ship. Dickson took only a few moments to record an entry. He noted, "All Friday and Friday night [we] had a pretty rough time of it in the Gulf [Stream]. A succession of squalls with hail and rain and thunder and lightning, straining and tumbling the <u>Standard</u> about pretty severely. It is said truly that it blows a gale of wind every day in the year in the Gulf [Stream]. At least so we have found it."

The gale blew itself out that night, and the morning of 29 March dawned bright and clear. It was at this time that the crew began to see signs that told them they were fast approaching the southeast coast and as a result entering the danger area of the Federal blockade. Suddenly all aboard realized that the purpose of their entire journey, the reason they weathered rough seas, short rations, and winter storms, was finally at hand. A few days' time would tell the story. Dickson recorded,

This Saturday morning [a] fine clear sky. Wind southeast, sea smooth. Saw the difference in the color of water almost immediately. The deep blue that we have just passed astern strongly contrasting the green color we are now in. [While] denoting the soundings the line was distinctly drawn between the two colors. To the east were the black frowning clouds of the Gulf, now resting on the horizon astern of us. . . .

Hove the lead [line] from the bow sprit. Away it flew, down, down. As it reaches the quarter deck [it] touched [bottom] in 45 fathoms. Three cheers were given with a right good will [and] the yards were cheerily brought around. Three more cheers were given for the Standard as she again moved westward through the brine.

As Mr. Hutchinson brought the lead [line] up over the quarter, [Captain] Blanch hails him. "What have you got there, Mr. Mate?"

"Gray sand mixed with small shell, Sir."

Charts were examined, our exact position ascertained and the probabilities of making Fernandina or Brunswick. It was decided after each giving his opinion that we would run in to fifteen fathoms, when we would then haul up until dark when, if the breeze continued, we would run in to 5 fathoms, drifting about until early dawn, when if no lights were seen of any of the Blockading Squadron, we would make up into the first Sound with the morning flood [tide].

All were full of glee, [and] all our past troubles forgotten. The risks and dangers of running in were not even thought of. After our hard fare was partaken of, fourteen fathoms were got with the lead [line]. A sharp lookout had been kept from the Top Gallant and Top Sail Yard all morning so as to keep clear of any of those gunboats prowling about.

2 PM—Ship hove to, sails all bent up to the yards, Stay sails all down. Not anything exposed whereby we would unnecessarily draw attention, but everything [was kept] loose, every sail ready to hoist in an instant to fly from any approaching sail. No noise was allowed. We were all told off in case we should have to run for it. I was washing some shirts in a bucket of salt water when the report of a heavy gun was heard to leeward. Shortly [after] another and then another, but in spite of all our endeavors we could see nothing. No friendly trader passed us, not even a "coaster" relieved the horizon. This once busy coast was deserted. We alone were endeavoring to reach its hospitable shores on the errand of peace and friendship, whilst the continuous roar of distant cannon proclaimed some action

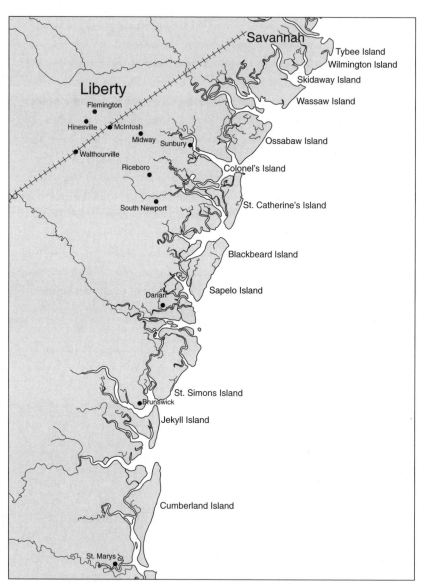

The Georgia Coast

between our batteries and the enemy's fleet. That we were in the immediate vicinity where war, fearful war, was raging in all its fury was evident, every gun of which we heard was perhaps playing its part in some bloody drama which would form a part of our future history. The deep, heavy roars' reverberation now [rumbles] almost incessantly over the ocean. The sea gull screeching in its fright flies rapidly to windward to escape the seeming danger.

About 3:30 PM the weather was slightly hazy. We were all startled from our dull inactivity by a cry from the lookout on the Top Gallant Yard. "A large steamer bearing right down on us through the haze, Sir!"

All fully realize their situation now. A thrill of intense pleasure, an excitement almost delirious animated me. All were moved with the strange emotion [of] wavering between success and capture. As soon as the "steamer" was seen from the quarter deck the orders followed in rapid succession. "Brace 'round the yards! Shake out Top Sail [and] Top Gallant sheet! Up! Up with the Fore Stay-Sail! All hands on the throat and peak of Mainsail Stay Sails, Gibs, Royal Gaff Top-sail!" Each followed in rapid succession in being spread to the breeze. In a few minutes we were under a perfect cloud of canvas flying over the waves to the westward. The Standard never looked more beautiful, certainly never done her duty more willingly as she rushed proudly on plowing up the sea at her bows in beautiful and ever changing banks of snow white foam.

The sudden threat of capture brought a new energy to the crew of the Standard. All were aware that sometimes the difference between capture and escape hinged on who saw whom first. At this point it looked as if the steamer had not yet sighted them, and the eyes of all aboard the Standard anxiously scanned the horizon in the steamer's direction. Dickson continued,

At first it was necessary to use the spy-glass to make her out plain but she was soon plain enough to be seen with the naked eye. The blockading steamer was running almost due south whilst a long black cloud of dense smoke arose from her smoke stack, floating far away over her stern until lost in the haze. She proved to be a propeller [ship] as she came more aft and had no doubt been one of the Crowell's Line that had been converted into a "Gunboat." We were now looking for a shot from her every minute, but no flash of flame shot from her sides. It was now evident that those on board were asleep, or that she must have been disabled on the coast with some of the batteries. Perhaps in the heavy firing that we heard during the morning in the nor-west. As the weather was now becoming every minute more thick, we soon saw the <u>Yankee Steamer</u> disappear amidst the haze and increasing the distance, much to our satisfaction.

The narrow brush with one of the blockading vessels was vivid proof that they were already on the outer fringes of the blockade and in danger of being seen by patrolling vessels. As a result a constant watch had to be kept from the masthead for the first sign of any ships. They cautiously pressed on for the southeast coast, so near, but yet still so far. In a few hours time a welcome cover of darkness cloaked them, which they hoped would allow them to come within sight of land by daybreak. Then they would make their dash for safety. That night Dickson wrote,

About 9 P.M. [We] hove ship to in seven fathoms, all hands on the lookout both from aloft and below for the lights of the blockading fleet or for any <u>gunboats prowling about</u>. Every precaution was taken to insure success and prevent detection. Both watches kept on deck all night, in fact no one thought of sleep. All orders given in a suppressed voice. Boards and canvas were nailed over all the dead lights, companion-way closed and covered to exclude a darkened lantern burning by the cabin. The binnacle light was even closed by a screen. Nor was a pipe allowed to be lighted on deck. Our position was frequently ascertained on the chart by dead reckoning. Of course we were drifting now up along the coast towards the nor-ward. We imagined that we would make, allowing for the opposite currents, about Brunswick, that is, the north end of Cumberland Island, at daylight. All of us felt feelings of gratification at the speedy prospect of our miserable condition being relieved, yet we were all anxious to a degree, as the long hours of the night passed wearily away.

The final drama of the *Standard*'s journey unfolded on 30 March as the vessel drifted along the Georgia coast near Darien. The purpose of the entire voyage was finally at hand. The men had suffered and labored through weeks of storms and privations, all for these next few nerve-wracking hours spent slipping through the Federal blockade. During the night the vessel managed to drift further into the blockaded area, and they hoped by daylight to be within sight of land. Dickson recorded the day's events in his diary as their harrowing journey neared an end.

> At ½ past 3 [A.M.] we could hear the breakers rolling in and dashing upon the beach to the westward, though only a few stars were to be seen amidst the somber-like darkness overhead. Five fathoms and a half. Wind not so strong as [we] might desire if a run is necessary.
>
> 4 A.M. Stood in, lead [line] going all the time. As day broke gradually in on us [we] could see through the glass the loom of the land. The British colors were immediately set <u>Union down</u> and a sharp lookout kept from aloft for any masts rising up against the loom [of land] ahead as the sun rose in all its glory. A haze to the eastward still favored us from passing vessels.

Daylight showed that the *Standard* was off Doboy and Altamaha sounds in the vicinity of Darien and gradually drifting northward toward Sapelo Island. There was still no sign of blockading vessels so the *Standard* proceeded cautiously onward to take a closer look at things. Dickson wrote,

> About 7 A.M. Made in for the north end of the Island the passage widening so [we] could not see the other side of the sound. The tide was again on the ebb and the wind quite light. Here we saw the absolute necessity of steamers alone attempting to run the blockade, as most frequently the very time you need the wind and its direction from the right quarter, of the most vital importance, it fails you, and a sailing vessel under such circumstances falls an easy prey to the enemy. It was now asserted by Tom that if the Latitude as taken the day previous at 12 [Noon] was correct the island ahead was Sapelo and we would be at the entrance of the Altamaha [River] and not far away from Darien, Georgia.

However, Tom Hernandez was mistaken, but not by much. It was something of a minor miracle that the *Standard* had even found the Georgia coast after having been blown so far off course several times during their journey, and it was perhaps to be expected that a small margin for error had to be taken into account. Up to this moment the vessel had been drifting off Sapelo Island, making its way northward for Sapelo Sound. But Hernandez assumed from his calculations that

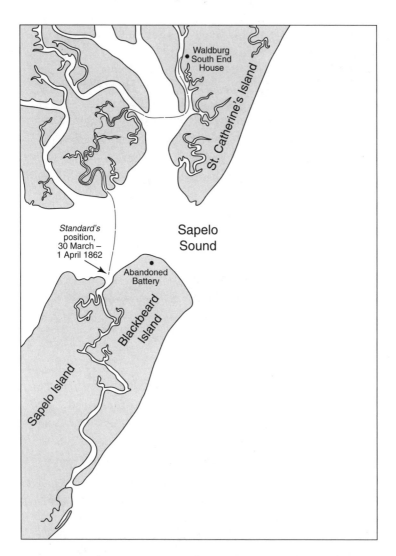

they were off St. Simons Island and approaching Altamaha Sound.
They were actually only a short distance north of where Hernandez
thought they were, but in navigating the coastal waters of Georgia,
an error of any small amount can bring about fatal results. Ignorant
of this mistake, the crew of the *Standard* continued the approach and
stumbled blindly toward the shallows known as Blackbeard Shoals off
Blackbeard Island. Dickson continued his narrative:

> What a lovely Sabbath morning. How suggestive of rest from labor,
> of praise for our deliverance from dangers at sea, yet it was not

Sunday on our brig, no rest for us. The atmosphere warm and balmy, the warm and genial rays of the sun rendering the very sea air fragrant with the verdue and bloom from the Island, even at this early period of the year. We watched with intense interest the long, low line of white beach as it stretched along until lost in the sea, covered with a dense foliage. All was quiet and serene, the sea rolling in slowly and breaking on the bar in foam, thence rolling in snow white surf upon the sandy beach. Occasionally some pelican would relieve the monotony of the scene by dashing down upon the water and with a peculiar shriek or cry, rise with its prey in its bill and rapidly fly towards land.

At 8:30 A.M. we were now in 3½ fathoms with the lead [line] constantly going. It was now quickly reduced to 3, 2½ and 2 fathoms and before we could get the brig around we were aground with the tide falling. Every effort was made to get her off, without avail. [The life] boat [was] sent all around the ship with the lead to sound but shoal water all around us and fast shoaling and almost in sight of the "Blockaders"! Finding all our efforts to no avail our vessel now liable to capture at any moment, an easterly wind threatening us with the flood tide, it was decided to take as much of the cargo ashore at once, as she would go to pieces on the flood [tide] if not gotten off.

Chests of medicine, drugs, teas and the men's clothes were at once placed into the boat [and] two double barrel guns, [a] bag of shot and [a] canister [of] powder. A piece of white shirt nailed upon a hand spike in our bows with a six penny handkerchief bearing the ensign of England in the stern [we] shoved off from the brig, 4½ miles to the Island. It seemed after all our trials the brig was at last to be wrecked, however not much time was left to regret the apparent fate of the brig or to sympathize with poor [Captain] Blanch, who deserved better luck. Although until carried away by other feelings more powerful [than] those of self-preservation, we felt it keenly.

Dickson and his companions were hopeful of making some type of contact with Southern forces, but they did not want to be mistaken for a landing party of U.S. sailors. They were unaware that the Confederate forces had abandoned all the offshore islands. Dickson continued:

With every precaution we approached the shore stopping several times and waving our flag of truce to prevent [our] being fired into by masked batteries or any leaden compliments being unceremoniously thrown into us by <u>Confederate Pickets</u>. We picked out a good place and at a favorable moment ran through the surf upon the beach unmolested [and] unharmed. The boat was speedily unloaded and . . . again shoved off for the brig, leaving Dugan, Tom and myself to carry the boxes and chests up the beach under the shelter of a low sand hill. No water had been brought ashore in the boat and it was thought proper to make a survey of our position before the boat returned and we might have the good luck to report to them the discovery of water or even perhaps some of the inhabitants. We accordingly armed ourselves with the guns, Tom taking the lead with the English flag in hand, we following in his trail Indian file.

The sun threw down its scorching rays upon us [as] we went several miles in as many directions. We met nothing but a wild and rank vegetation rising from a bed of sand as forbidding to us as the Great African Desert. We forced our way through thickets of [Spanish] Bayonet and Scrub Palmetto, plodded through ridges of hot, snow white sand nearly knee deep, waded across marshes, through cane breaks and reeds without discovering the first evidence of water or the signs of any inhabitants.

After several hours [of] severe toil we returned to the beach almost worn out. As we returned we found much to our satisfaction [that] the boat was running through the surf on her second trip to the Island. We immediately made known to them the result of our search and it was of course at once concluded upon that the Island was undoubtedly deserted by its inhabitants and evacuated by our forces. We were now to be on our guard for runaway Negroes who undoubtedly swarmed all [of] these Islands and [we] would perhaps have more occasions to dread them than the Yankees.

Our boat was well ladened down [with] chests of teas, bales of cloth, cases of boots, etc., charts, quadrants, papers, etc. All that had been brought ashore was a quart or two of water and a tin dish to bail with. It was decided now as the flood [tide] had again set in, to immediately set off for the brig to throw over part of the cargo and if possible get the brig off, drop anchor as soon as she floated, and then man the boat and take us off [the island] before morning. We [were] to keep up a good rousing fire on the beach during the night whereby they might ascertain our position in the darkness.

John Day was now left to increase our party to four and to act as our good man Friday. It was also made known to us that if the brig could not be gotten off they would remain on board until she went to pieces, which she would soon do if the wind, now northeast, increased, and save all that was possible. If surprised by any of the "Blockaders" they would set fire to the vessel and attempt to join us. They were not to delay sending us food and water a moment longer than was necessary. It was now Sunday afternoon and all we had eaten or drank since our frugal and scanty meal Saturday night was the small allowance of water now being dealt out. We had had no rest since Friday night having all hands been on deck the entire night, worked all day and were all but broke down. Still we were cheerful as long as the brig remained in sight.

We had now no time for thought, the boat was fast disappearing from view, on her return to the brig. We shouldered the guns and our party, four all told, went up the beach for drift wood, some of which we had seen in the morning. Several barrels were thus secured that had been washed up, [and] one box marked:

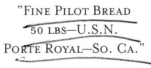

"Fine Pilot Bread

50 lbs—U.S.N.

Porte Royal—So. Ca."

[It] was as clean and new as if just from the carpenter. They had of course been thrown from the vessels of the fleet and carried by the current on the beach. The wreck of a large ship was nearly entirely buried or entombed in the sand about half a mile further along the beach. After several toilsome trips to the wreck we procured quite a supply of firewood [and] a roaring fire was lit.

While Dickson and his companions toiled on the beach of Black-beard Island to collect wood and get a fire started, back aboard the *Standard* the lifeboat was just returning from its last run to the beach, and efforts were begun to get the ship into deep water. Dickson wrote, "When they reached the brig, it was nearly high water. Immediately one gang set to work to throw over a number of barrels of salt that were got up from the hold. Another party took soundings about the vessel. A fresh easterly wind was now blowing. About sun-set all sail was made, and they succeeded in finally dragging over the outer sand bar into deeper water."

Back on the beach, Dickson and his comrades anxiously watched the vessel in the growing twilight. "As the brig was making sail we watched her with much anxiety. One [man] could see her move, another declared she was exactly in the same position. At last after some half hour she did move [and] changed her position towards us. Now we were in high glee as sail after sail filled out to the now freshening breeze."

Although the *Standard* was floating free after being dangerously exposed throughout the entire afternoon, all was not well. While James Dickson and his companions were rejoicing on the beach, the remainder of the crew aboard the *Standard* were reacting to another menace. "At this time the blockaders were in sight. They could not perhaps have seen [the *Standard*], the loom of the land no doubt obscuring her from their view, although the Federal's vessels were plainly visible. The course of the brig was now straight up the coast with a bright lookout ahead."

The rejoicing of those on the beach suddenly turned to consternation as they watched the *Standard* disappear to the north, stranding them there on the beach. Dickson noted,

> We could not account for the strange conduct of those on the brig. It was soon evident she was rapidly increasing the distance between us and with the growing twilight would very soon be out of sight. It was not long ere only a faint outline of her upper masts was to be seen and night soon visited [us]. The <u>Standard</u>, our "hope" [was gone] from sight. We did not believe for a moment that [Captain] Blanch and the crew would desert us and leave us on this desolate spot without food, water or a boat, even without an axe, with only our guns with a limited supply of ammunition, cut off by the sea from the mainland and surrounded by enemies and even unknown to our friends. Could our "brig" have run away from the Blockaders and they in pursuit or had they sent in boats to attempt to cut her out. The danger must have been eminent or otherwise to account

for their conduct would be impossible. One or the other cause was certain, either possible.

We were in much suspense in regard to the fate of the brig and listened attentively in the momentary expectation of hearing the roar of cannon from some one of the Federal's frigates, then we imagined by hearing no guns [that] she had eluded them in the darkness. Our own situation was then canvassed and at one time we were to abandon our charge at half ebb [tide] which would correspond to 2 A.M., direct our course by my pocket compass, to the creek some 3 miles to the north and cross it by fording and swimming before daylight [and] thence have a fresh days march before us. However this was reconsidered and very wisely, when the time approached, that it would be highly imprudent to move forward in the middle of the night none of us knowing where. Again it might be possible if the fire was well kept up, it might be the means of leading the brig back to our place of rendezvous, but most fortunately we agreed even at the last moment, to remain until morning to see if the brig would then be off the Island.

John set to work to boil our scanty supply of water in the tin pan whilst I broke open a chest of Bohee [tea]. Tom and Dugan arranged a sort of barricade with the bales and boxes around our sleeping place. After our tea had been drunk, more wood was procured for our fire [and] the guns reloaded with double charges. John and Dugan taking the first watch, Tom and I turning in to sleep until low ebb [tide] which would be about 12 [midnight]. We lay stretched each on a sailors chest, our only couch, the canopy of heaven our curtain. Yet soundly we slept until awoke to get more wood and take our place and watch, until daylight.

The scene was indeed strangely wild. A rare scene for the painter, as our huge fire shot upwards, shedding its lurid glare upon the white beach, on which broke the dull, heavy, unceasing roar of the Atlantic within a few yards of us; illuming the dark blade-like leaves of the [Spanish] bayonet tree of the tropics and our own fan-like Palmettos, and throwing its sickening glare on our little weary party. Yet on the alert for danger which seemed to lurk from every side around us. The wind was driving the spray and mist far inland, chilling and benumbing us with the cold and moisture. Beyond this little circle of light all was dark, dreary as the grave. So utterly overcome was I with fatigue, regardless of the dangers around us, I actually fell asleep with my gun in my hands. Regardless of the consequences we were soon roused up however [as] the tide was all around us. Boxes, chests, clothes, bales, everything had to be removed further inland.

We had not gone [far] until compelled amongst the palmetto scrub [despite] fear of <u>rattlesnakes</u> and <u>centipedes</u> which are as thick as blackberries on these islands. After much labor we succeeded in getting everything out of reach of the sea, but cold. I think I never felt it so severe, even on Cranberry Island [Maine]. The dew or mist was so heavy that it rolled off in big drips from my mackintosh. In spite of the great fire near us and heavy clothing we all shivered as if we had the ague.

John, during the night, was our main-stay, either walking around us or renewing the fire. John, poor fellow, made us all laugh by one of his quaint, rude remarks. "I have fight de Ingins in Canada, the niggers in de <u>West Ingies</u>, cheated them chaps de Esquimos, but I be damned if ever I seed such a bloody place as this before, at sea or on land. No, no, I'll keep my weather eyes open. Never fear me sleeping." Our position can be readily imagined. Our being fired into by Confederate pickets, surprised and shot down by the Yankees or our throats cut by the infernal runaway negroes on the Island for the sake of possessing themselves with what was around us.

The dawn of 31 March found Dickson and his companions still stranded on Blackbeard Island and disappointed to find no sign of the *Standard*. Dickson recorded,

Daylight at last broke in, the rising sun dispelled the mist and our brig no where to be seen along the horizon. We were alone. As I gazed upon the line of low, white beach not a sign of inhabitation, of welcome or friendship greeted us. To seaward all was the same, ever unchanging. No sail interrupted the line that bound ocean and sky together. The breakers rolled in on the shore amidst the same unceasing roar to within a few feet of our strangely wild encampment. Strange, dark foreboding thoughts of impending evil rushed upon us all. Our fate seemed already written to its fullest depths. We now felt the sad, dreary, word <u>alone</u>, yet we had been so often placed in extreme peril, we had become inured to danger. A philosophical fortitude to brave it out soared above despondency, thus it seemed we had become schooled even in our severest trials to struggle seemingly against fate.

A further survey of the island we now deemed totally unnecessary. Our supply of ammunition was limited and upon which rested alone our means of subsistence. It was therefore evident that the sooner we endeavored to reach the mainland the better, but the practibility of such an attempt was questionable. We had no tools even to cut down a tree, not even a hatchet having been brought ashore. To build a boat was impossible, but the ingenious, inventive knowledge of the sailor pointed to drift wood and bundles of cloth. Whether all or any of us would have succeeded in reaching the mainland if we had proceeded to such an extremity, God only knows.

Hunger now pressed upon us. It [was] now decided to immediately set about to procure food, after which we should decide upon what course to pursue, and immediately act upon the same. John Day and Dugan volunteered and set out with the guns, I turned in to get a little sleep, almost overcome with fatigue and want of rest, stowing myself between boxes and bales, my mackintosh wrapped about my head to keep off clouds of the most annoying of all insects— sand flies. As I lay down the crack of one of the guns was heard. Deluded with the prospects of a good breakfast I was very soon in the land of dreams.

While Dickson slept fitfully on the beach and the hunters searched for breakfast, other events were taking place elsewhere. The *Standard* had actually fled only a short distance north and taken refuge in Sapelo Sound. With the first light of dawn on 31 March, the ship's lifeboat was manned and sent out to try and locate the stranded party. Dickson slept for only a short time before being roused.

It was not perhaps nearly 9:00 A.M. The sun was shining brilliantly in the heavens when I was suddenly awakened by Tom. . . . "Jim, Jim! Here's the brig's boat, rouse up quick!" I could not realize the possibility of such an event. I doubted, disbelieved it, until I was almost dragged down to the beach, and sure enough, the [life]boat was about ¾ths of a mile outside the first breakers to the nor'east of us. Tom was delirious with joy. I was nearly, if not quite crazy. The crew [of the boat] were laying on their oars and were evidently in doubt about something. They hesitated several times about entering the breakers.

We shouted, ran up the beach and at last raised the Union Jack on a stick. A few seconds after, they saw us, as they took off their hats and waved them in token of recognition. The steersman arose in the stern sheets waving his hat with one hand, beckoning in shore with the other. Immediately they gave way and a second later were pulling lustily through the outer breakers. Dugan and John came up to the camp almost at the very instant the boat touched the beach. At that instant I verily believe we were more like escaped lunatics, than sane people. Men hugging one another, tears of joy actually coursing down weather beaten cheeks. Stern nature had given way and we had for awhile become children again.

Our story was related and amidst much laughter John Day wound up the narrative by producing a fearfully torn and mangled specimen [of] sandpiper, the joint production of our volunteer sportsmen, upon which a most incredible amount of ammunition had been used. Our fears were dispelled, our troubles soon told, but a short time was spent in relating their story. . . .

[The night before] as the entrance to the Sound was reached, [the Standard] had gone right up passing the northern end of the Island we were upon, and night had veiled her from our sight. They shortened sail, feeling their way up [the Sound] with the lead [line]. After going up some distance, the water rapidly shoaling, they let go both anchors. The sails were all furled and stowed, the hatches secured. As soon [as] the first dawn of day [showed] they placed a compass, part of a raw ham and jug of water in the boat. Taking the bearings of the ship they shoved off in search of us down the coast. On board they had worked all night like beavers, and as for food had done the same as ourselves—gone without. All hands had been most anxious on our account and as soon as possible set out to recover us, only Hutchinson and the cook remaining aboard. [Captain] Blanch now like us all, believed some good luck was in store for us.

No time was to be lost so the word was passed for all to bare-a-hand and bring down [to] the beach [and] into the boat the most valuable portion of what was on shore. We all turned Peter Williamsons,[6] carrying chests of tea, medicines, broken cases of cloth, bales of goods, our clothes, etc. nearly knee deep through the sand to the boat. [With] the surf rolling in, it was quite a job to load her. One party in the water had to hold her steady whilst we placed package after package in the yawl, wading out waist deep and woe betide you if you made a wrong calculation in regard to time and distance for if the sea broke on you it would bury you, load and all, in the cool brine, leaving you well dunked, and to get out the best way you could and a good laugh at your expense. Some most ludicrous scenes occurred. Each in turn was greeted with immense amounts of merriment and applause from all hands, excepting the nearly strangled victim, who as a matter of course, couldn't see the joke. Some of the less valuable, [and] more bulky articles were left behind, not being able to carry all.

Our Union Jack cotton handkerchief was given to the breeze as we shoved off. I was to steer so away we went through the breakers, fortunately for our over-loaded boat, all safe. It was a novel sight our boat and cargo, the heads of the men at the oars just visible above the pile of goods, a little party of three or four [men] in the stern perched on tea chests eating each his piece of fat, raw ham with a gusto quite enviable to despeptics.

Large numbers of cranes, curlews, pelicans were scattered along the beach. One of the latter, an immense bird, we wounded and succeeded in getting him in the boat. The bill and pouch or [the] maw, was very large. After rounding the island we kept close in shore, one of the men killing a rattlesnake with the oar. Shortly after the man in the bow reported that a man had disappeared into the thicket ahead, apparently on watch. However, we kept a little further out, some of us doubting his report. . . . We came in sight of the brig. We now were opposite to an abandoned battery.

The battery seen by those aboard the little boat was on the north point of Blackbeard Island. Abandoned by General Lee's orders after the fall of Port Royal in November, the battery had been left unmolested since then. Dickson and the crew of the *Standard* were not aware of these developments, and they hoped friendly Confederate soldiers might still be in the area. But there was no sign of life at the battery so it was decided to investigate further. Dickson wrote,

> One of the men jumped ashore and in a few minutes returned reporting everything completely capsized but a good well of water which we might avail ourselves of. A long pull across to the brig. When we reached her it was 2 P.M. the sun sending its rays down on us like a mid-summers day. We were all glad enough to put our feet on the <u>Standard</u>'s deck once more. Hutchinson greeted us warmly. "Well Dickson, God bless you. My 'eyes' eh! But I am glad to see you again. So you have had a pretty hard time of it, poor fellows."
>
> Poor Ben threw down his shovel to congratulate us on our safety. With a satisfied air of one who is aware of having done his duty, he pointed to an enormous pile of nicely browned Slap Jacks. "I knew as you would be most famished and I brewed you all a good mess of tea in the fluid can."
>
> This was cut short by <u>Hutchie</u>. "Come Ben rouse up there, D— your eyes, do you want the poor fellows to starve whilst you're reeling off one of your galley sermons?" This from the mate of course was a settler. As Ben's pile came beautifully less our story was told and retold and thankful were we that we had thus far been spared and by God's good care passed through so many trying scenes. I believe we all saw the hand of Providence in our being permitted again to be together and we took fresh courage and resolved to push our adventurous trip to a successful termination if possible.

After appeasing their hunger and thirst, all turned their attention toward finding a safe harbor for the *Standard*. Even though they had penetrated the blockade, they were still dangerously exposed and liable to capture or destruction at any moment. The first order of business was to find an anchorage that was safe from prying eyes and roving gunboats. The charts were pulled out and consulted. In spite of their recent difficulties, they were still unaware of their exact location and continued to rely on Hernandez's incorrect calculations, which would once again lead them into additional difficulties. Dickson continued, "Tom Hernandez thought we were off St. Simons [Island at] the mouth of the Altamaha River and about thirty-five miles from Darien, Georgia.

He being a Savannah Pilot, his opinion was at once accepted and preparations were at once commenced to proceed up the river and procure a pilot to take the <u>Standard</u> up to a place of safety."

Since the men of the *Standard* were still unaware of their exact location and had not questioned Hernandez's calculations, they decided to send out a party of men in the ship's boat to proceed upriver to Darien in hopes of locating a pilot who could guide the vessel to a safe anchorage. Until this could be done, the *Standard* enjoyed an extremely thin margin of safety, and time was working against them. Dickson noted,

A white flag was placed in the bow [of the ship's boat] and the English flag, a seven pence half-penny cotton Union Jack handkerchief in the stern. A tin pan of "slap jacks," a valise and a small carpet bag of mine and a small trunk of Tom's were put in our leaky boat. John Day, Fraser, Ben, Dugan, Tom and myself again left the "old brig" with a cheer and good wishes for [a] safe and speedy return.

After leaving the broad sheet of water in which the brig was at anchor we came into the river which like all the streams on the Georgia coast was very circuitous. As far as the eye could reach, marsh, marsh, marsh, not a house, boat or anything betokening an inhabited country could be seen. But we kept relieving each other at the oars, faithfully doing our duty.

After some two hours [of] hard toil, questions were put to Tom who acted as our pilot and steersman, if he knew or not, where we were, as we evidently [had] come into a cross stream or branch on which was part of a "beacon" we had passed some time before. A very unsatisfactory reply having been given by Tom, the men tired out as they were, lost their patience as well as their tempers. One of them attempted to strike Tom down with an oar and trouble we soon would have had but for my interference and Dugan's entreaties.

A long pull and it seemed as if we would have to sleep in the marsh all night. Salt water everywhere and our slap jacks gone. The sun had now set and as I stood up in the stern of the boat the rank marsh grass moved gently backward and forwards. Nothing to the west but an unbroken sea of cane and grass until bound by the golden sunset sky. To the left a small "Hammock" relieves the dreary waste. Here and there a few ducks rose before us and flew beyond our gaze; and now in coming sharply around one of the bends in the river a large white painted house partly hid in the dense foliage opened upon our delighted eyes.

On we pulled, the stream our guide. At one time [the house appeared to be] on the starboard quarter, another bend in the river and soon the "Mansion" would be off the opposite quarter of the boat. Again we would apparently be pulling directly from it and it right over the stern.

About dusk we came up to a wharf and opposite the house, which lay apparently inland about a mile. Making fast the boat we jumped ashore taking the two flags with us, I going ahead with Dugan carrying them. A few hundred yards over a kind of causeway we came to a stream. A small "bridge."

At this point the narrative of James Dickson's diary ceases in mid-sentence, in mid-page. Even though we may never know the end of the story from Dickson's perspective, there are pieces of the puzzle that do exist, and by putting them together the story of the *Standard*'s eventual fate continues to unfold. The "small 'bridge'" they reached crossed over a stream that cut through the causeway they traveled. Once across the bridge, they would have continued on the causeway a short distance

Remains of the causeway that Dickson, Hernandez, and their companions crossed on the evening of 31 March 1862. Photograph by the author and Lynn Holman.

A telephoto view looking back where the previous photograph was taken, showing the causeway remains. The landing where the Standard's boat was tied up was located to the right, just beyond the clump of bushes. Photograph by the author and Lynn Holman.

before reaching firm, high ground. The "Mansion" that Dickson and his companions were approaching, at the point where the diary narrative ends so abruptly, was the South End House on the southwest end of St. Catherine's Island. It was one of two plantation homes on the island, owned by Jacob Waldburg, a sixty-eight-year-old native of Savannah.[7] The island had been abandoned by the Waldburg family and all of the white populace shortly after the fall of Hilton Head, leaving only the older black people to fend for themselves as best they could. The black population of the island was already beginning to increase steadily as runaway slaves made their way across the marshes, rivers, and creeks, in search of the freedom that the islands held.

On that evening of 31 March, James Dickson, Tom Hernandez, Ben, Dugan, and Fraser were probably greeted as they approached by the black people who were living there. Dickson and his companions must have had a moment to pause and hesitate once they realized that theirs were the only white faces in the group. But the natives would have been friendly; for the most part they were old men, women, and children. In all probability the black community provided the haggard sailors with food, drink, and directions; and as the sun was setting, the group may have stayed the night, sleeping warily. On the following morning they could find their way back to the *Standard*, at anchor in the back reaches of Sapelo Sound to the south. However, with firm bearings, they may have attempted to return to the *Standard* in the evening darkness. There is no way today that we can determine their specific movement at that time.

FOUR

Results and Consequences

On the morning of 1 April 1862, James Dickson, Tom Hernandez, Ben, Dugan, and Fraser recrossed the causeway to the dock where their "leaky boat" was tied up and proceeded down Johnson Creek toward Sapelo Sound to the south. The day before, relying on Hernandez's calculations that they were near the community of Darien, they had proceeded into the Todd River, which they thought was the channel into the town. However, rather than leading to Darien as they expected, this stream narrowed as they ascended it and became a twisting, turning marsh creek. They must have been greatly surprised to learn their true location and that if they had just followed Johnson Creek north after leaving the vessel the day before, they would have found the South End House much sooner and much easier. Since they were not near Darien as they had assumed, their attempts to reach that place by using the map led them into the tortuous creek and cost them an afternoon of unnecessary effort. But it made no difference as they had made contact with local inhabitants and now knew precisely where they were.

The *Standard* lay at anchor in the back reaches of Sapelo Sound throughout the night while the crew anxiously awaited developments. On the morning of 1 April they were reunited once again. Now properly oriented as to exactly where they were, they consulted their charts and held a conference to decide the best course of action. They knew they were some fifteen miles north of where they had calculated the day before, and although having successfully penetrated the blockade, they were not yet out of danger of discovery by roving gunboats. They needed to get the *Standard* to a safe harbor somewhere, but where? First they had to make it safe from enemy eyes, then they could decide just where to take it. As it was, they were still far too exposed in the open sound. Sometime during this day the *Standard* was taken up Johnson Creek, past the South End House on St. Catherine's and into Waldburg Creek, anchoring off Waldburg's North End House on the opposite end of the island. The crew had communicated with the black people in this area and probably got a chance to vary their diet from the many "slap jacks" they had consumed in the past weeks, by bartering some of their cargo.

Since the blockade of the Georgia coast had been firmly established only a few months before, the U.S. Navy vessels were still unfamiliar with the intricacies of the inland waterways behind the barrier islands. The *Standard* was fairly safe, hidden from sight behind St. Catherine's Island. However, unknown to them, their margin of safety was extremely narrow. The blockade up to this point had consisted of cordons of ships that guarded the entrances to the major port cities. The *Standard* managed to slip through with relative ease or luck. However, following the successful capture of Fernandina and Jacksonville, Florida, Admiral Du Pont was only days away from establishing an inner blockade that would station at least one gunboat in each of Georgia's major coastal sounds. If the *Standard* had tried to slip into one of these sounds a few days later, the crew would have been unpleasantly surprised. But the men of the *Standard* never knew for certain just how closely they had courted disaster.

The morning of 2 April found the *Standard* still lying at anchor undetected, in Waldburg Creek off the North End House on St. Catherine's Island. To try and reach either Savannah or Darien would involve much intricate sailing through the inland waterway while under constant threat of discovery by patrolling gunboats. It was too great a risk for the distances involved since the men were unfamiliar with the waterways, and even Hernandez's piloting abilities may have been called into question. But to stay where they were any longer than necessary only invited trouble. The black people on St. Catherine's could not be trusted and could disclose the *Standard*'s location to the Federals at the first opportunity. The *Standard* needed to reach some place where the vessel would be out of sight and out of reach of the gunboats. Then it would be a simple matter of selling the cargo and securing another cargo. After that they would be faced with making a run through the blockade again.

In the immediate area, to try and go up the Medway River and further up the Jerico River would not put them out of easy reach of Federal vessels, and the channels farther up were too shallow. The North Newport River was close to the *Standard's* anchorage behind St. Catherine's Island and seemed to offer the safest haven. The wide channel of the North Newport wound casually through the marsh, then narrowed as it twisted inland. It was a difficult channel but still navigable. Before the war coastal steamers regularly made the run up the river to the little community of Riceboro at its headwaters. Captain Blanch probably hoped the twisting, narrow channel of the North Newport might serve as an effective barrier against detection and intrusion by Federal gunboats.

With their course of action decided upon, the crew of the *Standard* came to life. The anchor was hauled up, and the sails let out to catch the wind. They proceeded down Waldburg Creek and into the mouth of the North Newport, where they could catch the flood tide to carry them upstream. The river here ran deep, wide, and unobstructed. As they approached the green horizon of the mainland, they were spotted by Confederate pickets from the Liberty Independent Troop posted on Colonel's Island. With the British ensign at the peak to identify themselves as "friends," the *Standard* crept closer to Colonel's Island, hoping they would not be fired on by pickets who might mistake their intentions.

The North Newport passes the southwest end of Colonel's Island by making a wide, hairpin turn. The high, wooded riverbank along this turn was known locally as Half Moon Bluff. It is possible, even probable, that the crewmen of the *Standard* paused here to communicate with the Confederate pickets ashore. While the sharp turn at Half Moon Bluff provided a safe anchorage, the masts of the *Standard* may still have been visible above the trees of the island, and the location was easily accessible to enemy gunboats, so the crew would have pressed on upstream.

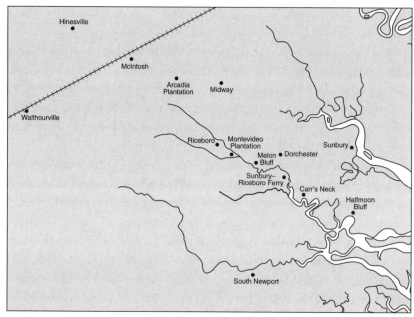

Liberty County

Once past Colonel's Island, the river narrowed, and varying tides, wind, and an uncertain channel made progress slow and difficult. A continual watch on the channel was necessary, and one man was constantly in the bow with the lead line to measure the water depth. When the tide fell, the *Standard* began hitting submerged sandbars and probably grounded several times. With luck, the men probably made it to a point where the river widened for a short distance just below Carr's Neck, where they could anchor until the tides changed and they could get a fresh days start. Although far enough upstream to be out of the way of prowling gunboats, they still needed to find a point where a landing could be made, as the marsh on both sides of the river presented a barrier to high ground access. Boat landings were located farther upstream, and, again with luck, they might make the docks at Riceboro. The next day would tell the story.

On 3 April the *Standard* probably continued its journey upstream after the flood tide reached them shortly after daylight. The crew proceeded past Carr's Neck, and a short distance further on passed within sight of plantations and a boat landing near the Sunbury-Riceboro ferry. Beyond that they passed another landing near the community of

Dorchester. As they traveled upstream, the river narrowed and twisted back on itself through the marsh. On the south bank they could see a cluster of buildings set back into the woods, which was the J. B. Barnard plantation, and they sailed past the landing that served it. The river continued to twist and turn, growing ever narrower.

It must have become evident that the *Standard* would not be able to make it all the way upstream to Riceboro so the men decided to anchor off the next boat landing, visible a short distance away, at Melon Bluff, near the plantation of Bartholomew A. Busby.[1]

The *Standard* was as far up the North Newport River as it could go, and the landing at Melon Bluff would prove to be the perfect place to unload their cargo and take on a new one. It was not really much of a bluff, as it was only a narrow neck of high ground that projected through the marsh to reach a bend of the river. Today we can only imagine the jubilation that must have been present aboard the *Standard* at this point. Their long journey, full of the dangers of stormy seas, against seemingly insurmountable odds, had finally been brought to a successful conclusion with a relatively intact vessel, crew, and cargo. It must have been a sweet celebration aboard the *Standard*. But there was still much to do. Arrangements had to be made to sell the cargo in Savannah, then unload it and transport it there and find a cargo for the return trip to Nova Scotia or some other port of convenience. It would probably take several days, if not weeks, to do this.

Bartholomew Busby, the seventy-four-year-old gentleman who owned the landing at Melon Bluff where the *Standard* had come to anchor, must have been surprised to find the vessel there. No ships of any size had come up the river since the summer before. Shortly after the *Standard* anchored off his landing, Busby probably received word of its arrival and went to communicate with the men aboard. He and his servants could provide all the information about the area that Captain Blanch needed as well as offering a source of manpower when the time came to unload the vessel. And so the *Standard* had completed its journey, but its story was far from over.

The presence of the *Standard* in the North Newport River would soon affect many people, particularly those who lived nearby. About two miles upstream from Melon Bluff, on the south bank of the river, was Montevideo Plantation, where the Reverend and Mrs. Charles C. Jones resided. The fifty-nine-year-old Reverend Jones was one of many planters who resided along the Georgia coast. Montevideo was about forty miles south of Savannah, in Liberty County, Georgia, and Reverend Jones owned and operated three plantations of considerable size. Arcadia Plantation, located about twenty miles from the coast and the largest of the three, encompassed almost 2,000 acres used for the cultivation of rice and cotton between Midway and Station Number 3, the railroad depot at McIntosh. Montevideo Plantation, located a mile and a half east of Riceboro on the North Newport River, comprised about 950 acres also used for those two crops. The third plantation was Maybank, a summer residence of 700 acres located on Colonel's Island, more suited for sea island cotton; the family resided here during the heat of the summer months when disease was rampant along the inland lowlands and ocean breezes provided some cooling relief. To operate these plantations, Reverend Jones owned 129 slaves, but he was not the typical master for he had devoted many years of his life to the evangelization of the slaves. This was recognized by all who knew him as the great work of his life.[2]

Reverend Jones had been educated at Phillips Academy and Andover Theological Seminary in Andover, Massachusetts, and Princeton Theological Seminary, where he graduated in 1830. He served as the pastor of the First Presbyterian Church in Savannah and professor of ecclesiastical history and church polity at Columbia Theological Seminary in Columbia, South Carolina. After this he served as the corresponding secretary of the Board of Domestic Missions of the Presbyterian Church, which had offices in Philadelphia, and then returned to his native Liberty County in 1853, where he supervised his plantations until the war intervened.[3]

He was married in December 1830 to his cousin, Mary Jones, and they raised three children, two sons and a daughter. They were a close-knit, loving family and were very supportive of each other and maintained contact through constant correspondence. The Jones's youngest child was Mary Sharpe Jones Mallard, who at the age of twenty-six was the wife of the Reverend Robert Q. Mallard, pastor of the Walthourville Church, located fifteen miles west of Riceboro.[4]

Their oldest son, Charles C. Jones Jr., a twenty-nine-year-old graduate of Princeton and the Harvard Law School, was serving as mayor of the city of Savannah when the war began. In July 1861 his wife and oldest daughter died of fever in Savannah, leaving him with an infant daughter. He left the child in the care of his parents and in August enlisted as a lieutenant with Capt. Joseph S. Claghorn's company of the Chatham Artillery, the state's oldest militia unit.[5]

Charles's younger brother, Joseph Jones, was twenty-eight years old and a graduate of Princeton and the University of Pennsylvania Medical College. He taught as a professor of chemistry at Savannah Medical College and as a professor of natural philosophy and theology at the University of Georgia. When the war came, he was serving as professor of chemistry at the Medical College of Georgia in Augusta. To his family he was affectionately known as "the Doctor."[6]

When the war came, Joseph left his wife and young son in Augusta and returned to Liberty County, where he enlisted as a private in the local militia organization, the Liberty Independent Troop, whose origins reached back to the Revolution. But Joseph found that his medical skills were in far more demand than his military abilities, and he was quickly appointed surgeon of the unit. The medical needs of his own unit, as well as neighboring ones and the local populace, soon took up much of his time.[7]

Reverend and Mrs. Jones had been living at Maybank Plantation on Colonel's Island when the war began, but after the fall of Hilton Head they relocated to Montevideo Plantation, up the North Newport River and just east of Riceboro. Although the river was navigable to the little community, it was thought to be safe from enemy gunboats since there was little to attract their attention. Through the following months life went on despite the war around them; however, it continued to close in upon their little piece of reality.

There was a great demand for labor to build defenses and fortifications, and Reverend Jones was as patriotic as the next Southerner, so he contributed his share of slaves for this work. However, when the slaves returned to the plantations, they brought back diseases they had been exposed to while in the military camps. The primary one was measles, which could spread rapidly and prove fatal. In no time a measles epidemic developed in the county, and Doctor Jones soon had his hands full. Reverend Jones watched with great concern as the disease began to manifest itself among his slaves.[8]

Rev. Charles C. Jones.
Courtesy of the Midway
Museum.

Montevideo Plantation House as seen in the latter half of the nineteenth century. Courtesy of
the Midway Museum.

When the *Standard* arrived in the North Newport River, Reverend Jones had a growing epidemic on all of his plantations. The blockade complicated the situation, since the necessary medicines were in short supply and quite expensive when they could be found. At this point in time, Dr. Joseph Jones's enlistment had expired, and while his unit struggled to reorganize under terms agreeable to its members, he was occupied with his medical demands. The unit reorganization was contentious, and until it was worked out, there was no organized military unit to cover the numerous picket posts along this portion of the coast. Thus, they were manned by volunteers. While these issues were sorted out, Doctor Jones kept busy tending to his father's sick slaves, as well as to many county residents.[9]

On that afternoon of 3 April, while the *Standard* was seeing its journey to a conclusion at Melon Bluff, upstream at Montevideo, Reverend and Mrs. Jones were pleasantly surprised by a visit from their eldest son, Lt. Charles C. Jones Jr. He had come only for a few days, but it was a welcome chance to visit his parents and spend time with his little daughter.

In all probability, on 4 April, Captain Blanch traveled to Savannah to make arrangements to sell the *Standard's* cargo. Since Dickson and Hernandez were natives of that city and Dickson's father had a business there, it is reasonable to assume that they accompanied him. There were a number of "commission" establishments in Savannah that handled the auction and sale of merchandise, produce, cotton, and so on for a percentage of the profit, or a commission. Their cargo would have found a "buyers" market and would have been in great demand.

From Melon Bluff they would have traveled west through Midway, past the Jones's Arcadia Plantation to McIntosh Station (Station No. 3), where they could catch the train to Savannah, about forty miles north. The Savannah, Albany, and Gulf Railroad provided rapid and convenient transportation for the *Standard's* cargo as the vessel was anchored only about ten miles from McIntosh Station. Local farm wagons could be hired to carry the cargo to the station, where it could be loaded on a train and carried to Savannah. For those of the crew who remained aboard the *Standard,* 4 April was probably a day of rest and relaxation. The little community of Riceboro, about three miles

Mrs. Mary Jones. Courtesy of the Midway Museum.

The children of Rev. and Mrs. Charles C. Jones. Seated left to right: Charles Jr. and Joseph. Standing at the rear is Mary Sharpe Jones. Courtesy of the Midway Museum.

Rev. Robert Q. Mallard and Mary Sharpe Jones with Mallard's mother. Courtesy of the Midway Museum.

Charles C. Jones Jr., mayor of Savannah, 1860–61. Seen here as a lieutenant in the Chatham Artillery, he was eventually promoted to command of Georgia State Artillery. Courtesy of the Coastal Heritage Society.

Joseph Jones, as a major in the Confederate Army. Joseph Jones Papers, Special Collections, Tulane University Library. Courtesy of Tulane University.

upstream, also would have offered some diversions for the crew and contact with the local populace.

About two miles upstream from where the *Standard* lay anchored on this 4 April, Reverend and Mrs. Jones were tending to the multitude of sick servants that had been struck down by measles at Montevideo Plantation. During the morning Wally, one of the suffering servants, died from the disease, the first fatality it had claimed there. This cast a pall of gloom over the whole plantation. Reverend and Mrs. Jones had plenty to hold their attention at Montevideo during this day and were probably unaware that the *Standard* had arrived at their neighbor's landing. But once the news got out, it would spread quickly throughout the surrounding neighborhoods.

James Dickson and the men of the *Standard* had fought their way through stormy seas and hostile gunboats to bring a cargo of much-needed medicines, commercial goods, and provisions to the Southern people. By 8 April they had probably made their arrangements to transport and sell the cargo. The firm of LaRoche and Bell, cargo auctioneers of Savannah, were engaged to handle the transaction, and now all that remained was to get the cargo to Savannah.

During this time many events were taking place on the Georgia coast that would have a great impact on the *Standard*. On the morning of 10 April, Federal forces on Tybee Island were preparing to reduce Fort Pulaski, where a resolute Confederate garrison remained firmly entrenched behind thick, masonry walls, guarding the entrance to the Savannah River. The fort had been isolated in February, and since then siege batteries had quietly been constructed on the northwest end of Tybee Island and heavy cannon manhandled across the marsh and emplaced in them. With the rising sun on 10 April, the Confederate garrison at Fort Pulaski discovered that the Federal batteries were no longer masked. A short time later, a demand was made for the fort's surrender, which Col. Charles Olmstead refused. Just after 8:00 A.M., the bombardment of Fort Pulaski began.

From the direction and intensity, most residents guessed that Fort Pulaski was the target. All along the reaches of Georgia's coastline people listened with uncertainty to the rumbling sound of the cannons. It was an unpleasant reminder of the war's reality on their doorstep. At Montevideo Plantation that morning of 10 April, Mary Jones took a moment out from ministering to the growing number of servants suffering from measles to pause and listen when the guns at Fort Pulaski resounded along the coast. About two miles downstream from Montevideo, the crew of the *Standard* were unloading its cargo at Melon Bluff. Forty miles to the south, the secret of the *Standard*'s arrival was being divulged to Federal officers aboard the USS *Alabama* at St. Simons Sound.

For the past few days a portion of the *Alabama*'s crew had been working with a group of black people in transporting a large amount of potatoes found at one of the island plantations two miles upstream. With the continuous influx of runaway slaves from the mainland, a small black colony was growing on the neighboring King Plantation, under the protection of the *Alabama*'s guns. The news of the *Standard*'s arrival in Sapelo Sound was carried to St. Simons Island by a black person from St. Catherine's Island. On 10 April, the news was carried to Cmdr. Edmund Lanier aboard the *Alabama,* and he reported it by dispatch to Admiral Du Pont.[10] He wrote, "Having heard this morning from an intelligent contraband that a schooner loaded with blankets, shoes, etc., had run into St. Catherine's some ten days since, and is now laying back of the island trading with the rebels, I intend sending an armed boat with orders to Lieutenant Commanding Watmough to take the schooner if safe and practicable."[11]

Lt. Cmdr. Pendleton Gaines Watmough commanded one of the many shallow-draft gunboats that enforced the blockade. He was a thirty-three-year-old native of Montgomery County, Pennsylvania, and considered to be an old navy man, having entered the service at the age of thirteen in 1841. After entering the navy, he served on the coast of South America, the Mediterranean, and the Pacific coast of the United States and aboard the frigate *Savannah* at Monterey, California. In 1846, when the Mexican War broke out, he participated in the capture of Monterey and later in the expedition to retake Los Angeles that culminated in the Battle of San Domingo Ranch. He entered the Naval Academy in 1847 and became a midshipman in 1848. After graduating, he cruised the Mediterranean and in the spring of 1852 served aboard the steamer USS *Mississippi* in Commodore Perry's expedition to Japan. In 1855 he was commissioned lieutenant and served on the coast of Chile, the coast of China, the Philippines, Japan, Java, and Siam. He returned to the United States in June 1858 and was ordered to the steamer *Michigan* to cruise the Great Lakes. In April 1859 he resigned his commission and entered private life.[12]

With the outbreak of war, Watmough traveled to Washington, D.C., and offered his services to Secretary of the Navy Gideon Welles. Appointed to the rank of volunteer acting lieutenant, he reported to Admiral Du Pont at the Philadelphia Navy Yard and served in the Chesapeake Bay area during the early weeks of the war. In May he was assigned as executive officer of the *Union* and was serving aboard that vessel when it initiated the blockade of the port of Savannah.[13]

Watmough commanded a gunboat during the attack on Hilton Head in November, participated in the capture of Beaufort, South Carolina, and then returned to Brooklyn Navy Yard to take command of the USS *Potomska*. The *Potomska* was a three-masted, propeller-driven steamer of 287 tons, measuring 134 feet, 6 inches long with a 27-foot beam; it drew about 8 feet of water and had a top speed of 10 knots. It had been purchased for the U.S. Navy from a George D. Morgan at New York

City for thirty-three thousand dollars on 25 September 1861 by an H. Haldrege and converted from merchant steamer to a blockade gunboat.[14] While they were at the Brooklyn Navy Yard on 17 December 1861, James Dickson and Tom Hernandez had passed by it while aboard the *Lilly Dale* as it passed up the East River on its way to Nova Scotia. After a number of delays, Watmough took the *Potomska* south to participate in operations along the Georgia-Florida coast. In February and March its crew was part of a task force that captured Fernandina, Florida, opened the inland route to Darien, and captured Brunswick, Georgia. Since that time, they had been on blockading station in Doboy Sound, east of Darien, Georgia. Ironically, on the night of 1 April, when the *Standard* was at anchor in Waldburg Creek behind St. Catherine's Island, the *Potomska* steamed by the island on its way to Hilton Head, unknowingly passing the *Standard* in much the same way the *Lilly Dale* had sailed by the *Potomska* four months earlier when it headed up the East River past the Brooklyn Navy Yard.

The *Potomska* returned to its duty station several days later, and on that evening of 10 April, the deck watch sounded the alarm on hearing a boat approaching from the direction of St. Simons. It turned out to be Acting Master John S. Dennis with a detachment of marines in an armed launch from the *Alabama* with Commander Lanier's dispatch for Lieutenant Commander Watmough.[15] It read,

> I have heard from contrabands that a schooner some ten days since ran the blockade and that she is now lying back of St. Catherine's, between that island and the main[land]. I have sent Acting Master [John S.] Dennis with 6 marines and an armed boat's crew, in case you may need their services. If you can go in the Potomska you may be able to take the schooner.
>
> I do not wish you to expose the boats where you can not cover them with your guns. I trust to your own good judgement to guide you in this affair, if you go. Your pilot will be able to inform you if you can get through with good water back of the island.[16]

Watmough conferred with his pilot over charts and maps of the area, and preparations were made to get under way as soon as the tides permitted. Perhaps there would be prize money if they managed to take the reported schooner.

Results and Consequences

In the early morning darkness of 11 April, the *Potomska* proceeded up the Mud River, bound for Sapelo Sound. By sunrise it was steaming across the back reaches of the sound while the lookouts scanned the horizon for any signs of the reported schooner. To the northeast lay the expanse of St. Catherine's Island, behind which the schooner had reportedly been seen several days before. Just to the southeast of the *Potamska* lay the north point of Blackbeard Island, where an abandoned earthen battery was noted.[17]

The *Potomska* proceeded up Johnson Creek toward St. Catherine's Sound, passing the wharf and causeway at the Waldburg South End House, where Dickson and the men of the *Standard* had landed two weeks before. With the sun rising in the eastern sky, the gunboat entered St. Catherine's Sound and anchored. There was no sign of the schooner, and Watmough examined the charts while lookouts scanned the horizon. While the *Potomska* lay at anchor, Watmough took the ship's launch and, accompanied by the armed boat's crew and marines, proceeded down Waldburg Creek to go ashore at the Waldburg North End House, which they had seen across the marsh on their approach. They were greeted by black people of various ages living there. Watmough questioned them about the schooner rumored to have been there. In his report he wrote, "We found that the brig, an English one, had passed there a week or ten days since, having entered at Sapelo, and from thence passed through the inland waters to Riceboro River (which goes inland from the head of St. Catherine's), up which narrow and difficult river she has been carried. They [the contrabands] say she had had a hard time and been obliged to throw overboard a portion of her cargo of salt; had lost her caboose, etc. That she was very deep, though I fancy she must have been a small vessel, as the river she went up only permits 7 or 8 feet draft and is full of difficulties, according to our pilot."[18]

Watmough returned to the *Potomska*, satisfied at having discovered where the schooner had gone, if not the schooner itself. The *Potomska* remained at anchor in St. Catherine's Sound throughout the morning. The rumbling guns at Fort Pulaski resumed their chorus, and it was apparent that the Confederate defenders were still holding out. While the *Potomska* remained in St. Catherine's Sound, at Melon Bluff, the cargo of the *Standard* was being unloaded for transportation to the railroad depot at McIntosh Station.

The arrival of the *Standard* in the North Newport River probably aroused some measure of excitement for those residents in the vicinity of Riceboro and Dorchester. The vessel was the first direct contact from beyond the blockade these people had experienced since the coastal steamers quit running the autumn before. There was much interest in the variety of goods and medicines that the *Standard*'s cargo comprised, especially at the Jones household, where medicines were in short supply and greatly needed to combat the growing measles problem there.

At Montevideo Plantation on the morning of 11 April, Mrs. Jones paused from her nursing duties among the sick servants and listened once more to the guns rumbling at Fort Pulaski. As a mother, she could not help but feel sympathy for other mothers and wives whose sons and husbands were bravely defending their homeland. She was proud that her own two sons were serving, but she could not help worrying at the continual sacrifices the war demanded. As previously mentioned, Joseph Jones had just finished his six-month enlistment and was presently helping deal with the measles epidemic.

Mrs. Jones's thoughts turned to her oldest son, Charles Jr., at Savannah. Then she remembered a letter she had started to him the day before and decided it was a good time to finish it. She wrote, "Our sick all better this morning: eight or nine cases up. The firing was heard again this morning, but the wind is so high and blowing from the west that we cannot now hear it if it continues. . . . The cargo of the Halifax vessel is fast discharging. I hope we may secure some of the quinine. Some persons suspect that it is a Yankee speculation; if so, I wish it could be proven, for it would nevermore leave our waters."[19]

Perhaps the rumor of the *Standard*'s journey having been financed by "Yankee" money was based on hearsay regarding James Dickson and Tom Hernandez having come from New York City. The quinine would indeed be welcome at the Jones plantations, if it could be acquired, especially in view of the measles epidemic, and even Reverend Jones was not in the best of health at this time.

That afternoon of 11 April, the *Potomska* moved into Waldburg Creek, past the Waldburg North End House complex, and into Johnson Creek, where it anchored. The launch and an armed boat's crew were sent on a reconnaissance of the North Newport River. They followed the channel upstream, taking soundings as far as Half Moon Bluff, then returned to the gunboat. About 4:00 P.M. the *Potomska* proceeded downstream bound for Doboy Sound.[20]

While the *Potomska* returned to its station at Doboy Sound, the drama at Fort Pulaski came to an end when Colonel Olmstead accepted the terms of a surrender agreement. There would be sadness throughout the South at another defeat, but there would be panic in Savannah when word of the fort's capture reached there. The Savannahians had confidently expected the fort to hold out as it was a powerful structure. However, just as with Port Royal the previous November, the fort did not live up to their expectations, and there was great distress. Their enemy seemed to be invincible.

The *Potomska* anchored in Doboy Sound about 5:00 P.M. that 11 April. Lieutenant Commander Watmough prepared a report of their reconnaissance for Commander Lanier in which he related the information obtained from the black people on St. Catherine's Island and other news.

> On Blackbeard Island we saw a deserted battery. There is also one on the south end of Sapelo [Island], which mounted five guns, with bombproof magazine. The lighthouse at this point is stripped and all the apparatus carried to Darien, according to contraband accounts. Yesterday we went up to within a mile or two of that town, but did not consider it safe to go farther, as the stream is narrow and we would have been left aground at half tide. We saw evidence of partial occupation of the neighboring houses and plantations.
>
> The islands are all deserted by the whites, who have left a few old slaves to care for things and shift for themselves. . . .
>
> Both St. Catherine's and Sapelo [sounds] offer fair opportunities for light-draft vessels to enter, and no doubt they reap a rich reward for their venture.[21]

That night Acting Master John Dennis with his marines and boat's crew left the *Potomska* in their launch bound for St. Simons Sound, carrying Watmough's dispatch to Commander Lanier.

Once it became general knowledge in Savannah, word of Fort Pulaski's fall traveled quickly along the southeast coast. Wherever James Dickson and Tom Hernandez were on this night, they were undoubtedly dreaming of the reward they would reap from their venture unless something drastic occurred in Savannah as a result of the panic caused by the fall of Fort Pulaski, such as the city's evacuation. After all the obstacles they had overcome to get there, nothing would stand in their way now that the concluding transaction was at hand.

The date of 12 April 1862 marked a milestone in the course of the war as exactly one year before, the conflict had begun with the bombardment of Fort Sumter by the Southern forces at Charleston. A year later it was Fort Pulaski's turn, and the roles were reversed. There were those on both sides who said the war would not last six months. Reality proved them all wrong, and now no one ventured to predict when the war would be brought to a conclusion.

At Doboy Sound, where the *Potomska* remained anchored near Doboy Island, 12 April dawned to overcast skies and inclement weather. At Montevideo Plantation, Reverend and Mrs. Jones were still tending to ill servants while their son Joseph ministered to those at Arcadia Plantation. Savannah was still astir at the news, and there was panic in some areas, although the military was resolved to hold the city against all attempts. At Melon Bluff the crew prepared the *Standard* for its anticipated return trip. Joseph Jones may have noticed the wagons passing Arcadia Plantation for the past few days that had been bearing the *Standard*'s cargo to McIntosh Station.

By 12 April the cargo was at the depot, where it was loaded on a north-bound train for Savannah. Once there it was hauled to the warehouse of LaRoche and Bell on Bay Street and inventoried prior to sale. On the morning of 14 April, the *Savannah Republican* newspaper hit the streets, and anxious readers scanned the pages for the latest war news. In the classified section in the back of the paper under the heading of "AUCTIONS," the following advertisement appeared:

BY LAROCHE & BELL CARGO SALES

To-Morrow, Tuesday, 15th instant, at 11 o'clock on Bay Street, three doors west of Abercorn, the entire cargo of the brig _____, from _____, consisting of the following articles:

500 bbls Turk Island Salt		5 Boxes Starch
25 " Mess Pork		200 lbs Pickled Herring
4 " Prime do		25 " Mess Beef

7 bbles Straw Seal Oil	7 lbs Cod Oil
40 boxes Cod Fish	8 " B.S. OH
200 " No. 1 Herring	16 tubs choice Butter
200 " scaled do	3 bbls No. 1 Salmon
18 boxes Raisins	3 " Salmon Trout
50 " Soap	24 Chests Tea, assorted
20 kegs Saleratus	2 hi bbls Ground Coffee
15 boxes Cream Tartar	6 boxes " "
2 " Saltpetre	6 kegs Carb. Soda
3 lbs Opium	14 ounces Quinine
7½ lbs Calomel	20 lbs Tartaric Acid
4 cases stout Brogans	1 doz Seidlitz Powders
4 cases Women's Shoes	49 m Military Gun Caps
and Brogans	3 tierces Hams
47 Bags Shot	27 gross Matches
5 boxes Ass'dd Spices	2 cases Box Table Salt

With figs, Mustard, Candles, Tubs, Pails, Brooms, and a various articles.

ALSO

10 cases desirable and seasonable Dry Goods, selected expressly for this Market

All of these items were scarce since the blockade had been established, and with the recent fall of Fort Pulaski, demand for these things would be even greater. One wonders why the name of the *Standard* and its homeport were left blank in the advertisement. Perhaps for the sake of security lest the knowledge of the ship's location fall into the wrong hands. However, unknown to the crew of the *Standard,* the Federal Navy was already aware of its location and were discussing the possibility of pursuit.

The following day, 15 April, the *Savannah Republican* carried the same auction notice in the classifieds, and in another section carrying announcements, they noted,

AUCTION SALE—An assortment of articles very much needed, and just imported, will be sold at auction this forenoon by Messrs. La-Roche

& Bell. The demand will doubtless be great and the bidding lively. Sale on Bay St., three doors west of Abercorn.

The crowd probably began gathering at the LaRoche and Bell warehouse on Bay Street well in advance of the 11:00 A.M. commencement of the auction. It is possible that James Dickson, Tom Hernandez, and Captain Blanch were on hand. Lieutenant Jones came from Camp Claghorn to see if he could obtain some quinine for his mother, who had expressed that desire in a recent letter. The auction probably continued throughout the day. Bidding must have been quite brisk and every item sold. The demand for medicines was especially great, and Lieutenant Jones was unsuccessful in his attempt to procure some of the quinine, so he returned to camp.[22]

During that 15 April, while its cargo was being auction, the *Standard* remained at Melon Bluff. However, its ultimate fate was being sealed at Port Royal, where Admiral Du Pont issued orders to Cmdr. John R. Goldsborough to take the USS *Florida* and assume command at St. Simons Sound. The order read: "You will please proceed with the least delay in the Florida to St. Simon's Sound and take charge of its blockade and of the surrounding waters extending to the northward as far as St. Catherine's, where I learn, a small vessel lately succeeded in entering, between these points on the Altamaha, Doboy, and Sapelo, which will have to be looked in to."[23]

A year earlier, Goldsborough had been the commander of the steamer *Union,* which initiated the blockade of Savannah in May 1861, and Pendleton Watmough had been his executive officer. Watmough had then assumed command of the *Union* when Goldsborough was reassigned. Events would now bring them back together once again.

At Montevideo Plantation on 15 April, Reverend and Mrs. Jones still had their hands full with the measles epidemic. Most of the sick servants seemed able to recover, but there were a few troubling cases. They took heart in the fact that there had been no new cases, and they saw this as a hopeful sign. Joseph Jones departed that day to accompany his wife and young son on their return trip to Augusta. They had been visiting Montevideo since January so they could be close by while Joseph served with the Liberty Independent Troop. However, the spreading outbreak of measles in the county was a growing concern for Joseph, and he thought it best that they return to Augusta while he remained to fight the epidemic, even though his enlistment had expired. He traveled with his family to Millen, Georgia, and then returned to the coast to help his parents.

The *Potomska* had been at St. Simons Sound since 14 April, where it was being recoaled and resupplied. On the morning of 16 April, it departed under orders to investigate a barn at the Spalding Plantation on Sapelo Island, rumored to hold a large amount of corn. The growing colony of runaway slaves at St. Simons placed a strain on available food supplies so Commander Lanier hoped to recover any useful provisions.[24]

At Montevideo Plantation on that evening of 16 April, Mary Jones wrote to her son Charles to update him on the state of affairs.

> Today another deep sorrow has fallen upon our household in the death of poor Joe. . . . He was one of the three who returned first from the fortifications; and although he looked badly, he went about until a week or ten days since. Your brother [Joseph] has felt very uneasy about him from the first, but did not anticipate his death when he left yesterday. His case has been very peculiar; I never knew any like it. . . . He died this morning at 10:00 o'clock.
>
> Our old servant Niger continues very ill; unless relieved shortly I see very little hope for him. Tyrone is still very sick; Adam a little better. Some eight or ten other cases; most of them measles. All the men who worked on the fortifications excepting Pulaski seem to have taken some poison from water, food, or atmosphere into their systems which defies the ordinary remedy. The effect of this increased anxiety and sorrow upon your father is very evident.[25]

On the morning of 17 April, the gunboat USS *Wamsutta* arrived at St. Simons Sound. Its story was much the same as those of many other gunboats operating on the Georgia coast. The *Wamsutta* had been purchased in September 1861, in New York City, from the same George D. Morgan by the same H. Haldrege as the *Potomska*. The Federal government paid twenty-seven thousand dollars for the 270-ton propeller steamer. It was of similar dimension and capabilities as the *Potomska* and for all practical purposes was identical to the other vessel.[26]

The *Wamsutta* had been sent to Philadelphia for outfitting and armed with four 32-pounder cannon and one 20-pounder Parrott rifle on a forward-deck pivot.[27] On 14 March the vessel was commissioned and departed for Port Royal. However, a storm opened severe leaks in the hull, and the ship had to return to Philadelphia. After repairs it proceeded to Port Royal, arriving on 14 April.[28] Shortly after its arrival, a new commander boarded the gunboat. He was Lt. Cmdr. Alexander A. Semmes. Semmes was a handsome figure of a man, tall, ramrod straight, with piercing steel-blue eyes, a stern jaw, and bushy mutton-chop whiskers.

He was a forty-year-old native of the District of Columbia and had spent twenty years in the navy. He witnessed the abandonment of the U.S. Navy Yard at Norfolk, Virginia, in April 1861 and had been commanding the steam transport USS *Rhode Island* since that time.[29] With command of the *Wamsutta,* Semmes hoped to see some active service. He wasted little time in taking the gunboat to St. Simons Sound, where it would be assigned a station in the blockade. Thus, on the morning of 17 April, Semmes brought the *Wamsutta* to anchor near the *Alabama* in St. Simons Sound and reported himself and his vessel ready for duty. The USS *Florida* arrived in St. Simons Sound on 18 April, with Cmdr. John R. Goldsborough aboard with orders to relieve Commander Lanier and the *Alabama*.[30]

During this time the *Potomska* was anchored off Barn Creek near the Spalding Plantation on the south end of Sapelo Island, about fifteen miles north of St. Simons Sound. A landing party sent to find corn confirmed that it was stored there, but it was still on the cob and would require shelling before it could be taken to St. Simons Island. A corn sheller was located, and soon the crew was organized into working parties to begin shelling, bagging, and loading the corn aboard the *Potomska*.[31] There was enough work to keep them busy for several days, although it was not exactly the type of blockading duty they had envisioned when they went to war.

At Montevideo Plantation on this 17 April, Reverend and Mrs. Jones continued tending their sick servants. Joseph Jones tried to help in any way he could while he pondered what course of action he would take in the coming days. The impasse within the ranks of the Liberty Independent Troop had not yet been resolved, and until that was taken care of, the question of reenlisting had to wait. He did know that the measles epidemic on his parent's plantations required his immediate attention. The one servant, Joe, had died while Joseph had been away escorting his family back to Augusta, and indications were that several other servants were in danger of the same fate.

By 19 April the *Potomska* had two day's worth of shelled corn stored below decks. The vessel departed Doboy Sound that morning, bound for St. Simons Sound to deliver the corn, as well as four black people from Sapelo Island who wished to go to St. Simons. The vessel took the outside passage, rather than picking their way through the inland route. About 11:00 A.M. the lookouts sighted a sail to the southwest, and the alarm was sounded. The crew manned their battle stations, and the lookouts strained to make out the details of the other ship. Within an hour they were close enough to make signals and discovered that the other ship was the *Alabama,* carrying Commander Lanier from St. Simons Sound to Port Royal. The two ships parted company after a brief exchange of signals.[32]

Lt. Cmdr. Alexander A. Semmes, commander of the U.S. Navy gunboat Wamsutta. *Courtesy of the National Archives.*

A short time later, another sail was sighted approaching from behind, so the *Potomska* heaved to as the lookouts watched the other ship. The schooner *Willie* soon came alongside, and a check of its papers showed it to be en route from Port Royal to Fernandina with a cargo of coal.[33] Since all was in order, the two vessels proceeded, each going its own way. The *Potomska* was still looking for its first capture.

By sunset the *Potomska* was anchored in St. Simons Sound with the *Florida* and the *Wamsutta*. The four black people were put ashore on St. Simons Island, and a short time later Lieutenant Commander Semmes arrived aboard from the *Wamsutta*.[34] Semmes and Watmough knew one another, both having entered the Naval Academy the same year and having graduated in the same class. Their meeting at St. Simons Sound was probably an interesting reunion, and the two men must have conferred about the situation on the coast and discussed plans for the *Wamsutta*'s eventual movement to its station. Watmough was also reunited at this same time with his former commander from his early war days on the steamer *Union*, Cmdr. John R. Goldsborough, who was there aboard the *Florida*.

The twentieth of April dawned as another fine spring day on the Georgia coast. At St. Simons Sound the crews of the *Wamsutta* and *Potomska* worked to unload the corn brought from Sapelo Island. During this time, up the coast at the North Newport Parade Ground, near Riceboro, the members of the Liberty Independent Troop gathered for their third meeting to try and effect a reorganization of the unit. It was hoped that this meeting would have more success, for without the unit their coast lay virtually unprotected.

Once the meeting was called to order, the men immediately got down to business. Since a faction that wanted to reorganize under the name of "Liberty Rangers" would not yield in their demands, there was only one course of action to take. Lt. William A. Fleming wrote, "We again met, and the Old Liberty Independent Troop was reorganized by electing William L. Walthour Captain. . . . The disaffected [faction] withdrew entirely from the meeting, thereby dissolving all connection with the company. In the mean time the members retaining the name of the Company and their arms, by volunteer detachments, kept up the picket-posts on the coast. And it was mutually agreed with the disaffected members, that should any demonstration be made by the Yankee Gunboats to enter the river, that a signal be given by firing of an old cannon at the Headquarters, Riceboro."[35]

And so the Liberty Independent Troop broke into two groups, neither able to muster enough men to form a company that could be enlisted into Confederate service. The disaffected group elected their own officers and formed the Liberty Rangers. Both groups would need to focus their efforts on enlisting new members to fill their ranks until they had the requisite number to go back into active service.

The *Potomska* and *Wamsutta* departed for their respective duty stations on 21 April. Commander Goldsborough instructed Watmough to take up his station at Sapelo Sound, while Semmes would assume the *Potomska's* previous station at Doboy Sound. This meant that the *Wamsutta* would assume the responsibility of recovering the corn from Sapelo Island, a duty that the crew of the *Potomska* was probably happy to let them have. By 2:00 P.M. both ships were anchored off the Duplin River at the south end of Sapelo Island.[36]

At Montevideo Plantation on that afternoon of 21 April, Reverend and Mrs. Jones and their son Joseph were still tending to sick servants. Joseph was increasingly burdened since his skills as a physician were greatly in demand by other county residents, which kept him traveling a good deal. The measles continued to be a growing problem, made more difficult by the lack of suitable medicines. They had hoped to obtain some of the quinine brought in by the *Standard,* but Lieutenant Jones was unable to purchase any at the cargo auction in Savannah. He wrote to his parents on the nineteenth: "Only fourteen ounces of quinine were brought by the vessel, and these were sold at fifteen dollars per ounce at public outcry. So soon as I can purchase any, you shall have it. A scarce article."[37] Reverend Jones responded in a letter to his son written on 21 April:

> The sending of our men to work on the Savannah River batteries has been a sad thing to us. Poor Joe died on the 16th with dysentery (river cholera) contracted there, making two of our best men. . . . Tyrone has been extremely ill; is still in bed and something better. Little Adam is just walking about. July has been very sick, and is barely convalescing. Sam was very sick for a short time. . . . The plantation, with these extreme cases and the measles with the people, has been on three weeks a hospital; and had not your brother

been with us, I do not know what we should have done. Arcadia is also suffering from measles; the men who went to Savannah have suffered much also. . . .

Your Brother . . . has had his hands full . . . between Montevideo and Arcadia. . . . It is a great interruption to him. He has not settled down on any plan for the future, and cannot until he returns to Augusta. The Liberty Independent Troop has split into two companies, neither sufficient in numbers to be mustered in; Lowndes Walthour captain of one, and William Thomson of the other. [Captain] Winn thrown out by both sides.[38]

On the morning of 22 April, the *Potomska* departed for its new station in Sapelo Sound. The crew of the *Wamsutta* had spent their first night on blockade, and they were not disappointed as during the night four runaway slaves in a small boat approached the gunboat. They were allowed to come aboard, and Lieutenant Commander Semmes questioned them and placed them in a room until he could determine what to do with them. When Lieutenant Commander Watmough heard that Semmes had picked up the runaways that night, he asked for them to be sent to the *Potomska* to serve as guides. Before the *Potomska* departed, the shelling machine used on the corn stored at Sapelo was sent to the *Wamsutta*.[39]

The *Potomska* arrived in the back reaches of Sapelo Sound about 3:00 P.M. that 22 April and anchored in English Narrows, southwest of St. Catherine's Island. Confederate pickets from the Liberty Independent Troop, located on Colonel's Island, saw the *Potomska* across the expanse of marsh and water and kept a close watch on its movements. There was no reason to sound the alarm, but this was the second time in as many weeks that a Federal gunboat had made an appearance in their area, and the presence of this enemy was cause to be concerned.

As the sun crept over the eastern horizon on the morning of 23 April, the *Potomska* left Sapelo Sound and proceeded north through the inland passage for St. Catherine's Sound. After grounding on a sandbar that morning, it steamed into Waldburg Creek, where it anchored off the North End House about 1:30 P.M. Watmough communicated with the black residents gathered at the edge of the bluff. They confirmed that no other vessels had been seen in the area since the *Potomska*'s visit on the eleventh. Watmough was certain the blockade

William A. Fleming and his wife. Fleming, a member of the Liberty Independent Troop, wrote a history of the troop in which he recorded the events surrounding the Standard's destruction. It was this information that started the chain of events that eventually lead to James Dickson's diary. Courtesy of the Midway Museum.

runner was still up the North Newport River, and, with a fresh start in the morning, he would see about ascending that river.[40]

At sunrise on 24 April, the *Potomska* steamed up the North Newport River and anchored below Colonel's Island. While the sun rose full in the eastern sky, the lookouts in the ship's rigging studied the treeline ashore to see if their presence precipitated any activity. Shortly after 9:00 A.M., two boats were lowered and crews detailed to ascend the river and sound the channel, but to return to the ship if they were discovered by anyone ashore. These boats departed about 9:30 A.M.[41]

Colonel's Island had been almost totally abandoned other than a few picket posts manned by members of the Liberty Independent Troop. The pickets on duty at Maxwell Plantation on the eastern end of the island saw the *Potomska* come to anchor but did not observe the two boats leave the vessel. Lt. William A. Fleming wrote, "At this time privates G[eorge] F[rederick] King, Roswell King [III], J[ulian] C[larence] King and Corporal A[ugustus] M[unroe] McIver were on post at Maxwell's Point. Early on [Thursday] morning they discovered a barge fully manned ascending the river and making soundings. As soon as the pickets were seen by them, they put around and returned to their boat."[42]

The pickets saw that the gunboat remained anchored out of range and showed no activity that might indicate an attack, so there was no cause to sound the alarm. Yet the fact that an enemy vessel had returned to the area and exhibited an interest in their river was not a comforting thought. Perhaps an attempt would be made to land troops along Half Moon Bluff.

The *Potomska*'s boats returned about 1:30 P.M., and Watmough learned from the man in charge that the channel posed no immediate problems but that they had been seen by Confederate pickets. Since the day was half gone and the tide was falling, Watmough decided to wait a day to ascend the river. He had no idea how far upstream the blockade runner lay, and he did not want to get aground upstream with night coming on, so they remained anchored off Colonel's Island.[43]

The *Standard* was still anchored off Melon Bluff, unaware that danger was so near. At Montevideo Plantation there was sadness as another servant, old Niger, died from the measles. He was the third servant the Jones family had lost in as many weeks. No one suspected that the calm routine of their lives was about to be shattered. As the sun set upon coastal Georgia, it was as if the house lights were going down to bring on the darkness before beginning the last act of this small drama.

⊷⊶ FIVE ⊶⊷

Time to Pay the Piper

bout 9:00 A.M. on 25 April 1862, the *Potomska* raised anchor and steamed up the North Newport River. On Colonel's Island, Confederate pickets reacted when the gunboat approached their positions. Lt. William A. Fleming wrote that the gunboat "proceeded to ascend the river, very carefully. Corporal McIver was immediately dispatched to Riceboro to give the alarm, by the firing of the old cannon."[1]

Shortly after 11:00 A.M. the *Potomska* anchored below Half Moon Bluff just off Woodville, Audley M. King's plantation. The lookouts carefully examined the long, sweeping, hairpin bluff but could see no signs of life. However, unseen eyes peered back at the ship from the underbrush near the King house as the Confederate pickets watched the vessel. They were not certain if it was going upstream or would eventually retire. If the gunboat did proceed upstream, they did not know whether to fire on it or not, since firing on the gunboat might only invite trouble. However, others felt it their duty to fire on the gunboat, as their reputations demanded it. Heated discussions arose among some of the men as they eyed the anchored gunboat. Aboard the *Potomska,* Lieutenant Commander Watmough sent a boat's crew and his pilot to Doboy Sound to summon the *Wamsutta* since he felt that with their assistance he could safely ascend the river. The boat departed about noon, and the *Potomska* remained at anchor.[2]

It began as a typical spring day in Liberty County, but the sudden threat of an approaching enemy changed everything. The alarm was sounded ashore, and residents who lived along the river and on Colonel's Island began to evacuate the area as there was fear of a possible landing of enemy troops. At Montevideo Plantation, Mary Jones was tending the sick and minding the daily affairs of the place when word arrived that a Federal gunboat was anchored off Colonel's Island. Reverend Jones wrote later to his eldest son, Lieutenant Jones: "The news came up from the Island . . . that . . . the enemy's gunboats were in Woodville River at Drum (Timmon's) Point below Mrs. King's place; that a part of the Troop under Captain W. L. Walthour had gone down to give them a brush should they attempt to land troops or come up the river; and that citizens were going down to aid. Your brother [Joseph] was at Arcadia [Plantation] visiting the sick when he heard it, and posted back to Montevideo."[3]

Joseph Jones was en route to Arcadia Plantation to tend to the sick there when he got word of the alarm. In a letter to his wife, he wrote,

On my way to Arcadia to visit the sick, I was informed that a Yankee Gun-boat was lying at Woodville and that the citizens and troopers were hurrying down to prevent the Yankees from landing. I hurried on, attended to the wants of the sick, and returned to Montevideo, gathered my private arms and ammunition, packed my saddlebags, mounted my horse and hurried down to Colonel's Island. On the way I received various conflicting reports about the movements of the enemy from the servants along the road. I met the wagons of Dr. Harris several miles beyond Riceboro, and Father's with the negroes from Maybank and still farther on one of Uncle William's carts—these all confirmed the report that the Yankees were making a demonstration upon the Island. The last servant which I met affirmed that the enemy had landed on Colonel's Island near Aunt Susan's house[4] and that our men had thrown away their arms and were in full retreat.[5]

When the *Potomska* lowered its boat and sent it off to summon the *Wamsutta*, Confederate pickets probably thought the Federals were preparing to come ashore. Thus, an alarm to that effect spread, and apparently the Confederate defenders from the Liberty Independent Troop decided not to remain and see what they thought was to be a landing of enemy troops, much less oppose it. They soon found this not to be the case, but word of an enemy landing spread like rings rippling across the surface of a pond.

While events unfolded on the coast, others entered the fringes of the developing drama. James S. Warnell, a thirty-one-year-old native of Walthourville, was reporting for duty with the Liberty Guards, the Liberty Independent Troop's sister unit. He wrote that he "left home . . . with a heavy heart" and traveled to the county seat of Hinesville where the new recruits were gathered prior to being marched to the Guards' camp on the South Newport River, below Riceboro. When the group arrived at Riceboro, they found the war much closer than they imagined. Warnell recorded in his diary on this 25 April:

> We heard in Riceboro that the enemy was on Cols. Island. The writer with several others wanted the Independent Troop to arm us and let us go to where we understood they were fighting, but was refused. We received intelligence at the boro that the enemy was near our camp and that the picket was out waiting and watching [for] our arrival. Arrived at So[uth] Newport River [where] we was welcomed by [a] picket. The picket [just] returned from out[post] and [he] reported the company safe [and] all in high spirits.[6]

While the alarm was spreading across Liberty County throughout the afternoon, the *Potomska* remained quietly at anchor off Half Moon Bluff. Aboard ship there was little to indicate the panic and alarm the sailors' presence had stirred throughout the surrounding countryside. About 5:30 P.M. the *Potomska* proceeded upriver, passing around Half Moon Bluff and steaming out to Crosstides Creek, where the North and South Newport rivers joined channels before separating again, where they anchored about 6:30 P.M.[7]

Joseph Jones arrived on the scene just before the *Potomska* steamed upriver to its anchorage at the Crosstides. He wrote,

> I urged my horse on as well as his strength would permit and reached the road leading to Woodville about 4:00 P.M. Here I found the horses of the men hitched and guarded by two of the Liberty Independent Troop. I dismounted, tied my horse, and commenced to load my gun. I had not completed this before I heard the sound of horses feet and in a moment the troopers came in full retreat saying that the Gun-boat was then passing Mrs. King's landing—

and that they had determined not to fire on the men [aboard the vessel]—We hastened back to Half Moon Bluff, and found that the boat had passed and was laying at anchor entirely out of reach of the Carbines and shot guns. I immediately urged upon the Troop and armed citizens the importance of sending a strong force to Carrs Neck, the only bluff and wooded land immediately on the river between Colonel's Island and Riceboro, where an effective stand might be made on this side of the river; and also urged the great importance of sinking in the channel of the river the vessel which ran the blockade, two or three weeks ago, and which was supposed to be the cause of the visit of the Gun-boat. After much discussion a party [of soldiers] was sent to scuttle the vessel.[8]

At Melon Bluff the day dawned like any other, but by the time the sun was sinking into the western sky, the situation would be altered considerably. The *Standard*'s crewmen probably heard that an enemy gunboat was in the river, and one can imagine the frustration and disappointment felt by Captain Blanch and his crew. The *Standard* was trapped. There was no place to hide if the gunboat came upriver. The only alternative was capture or destruction.

Joseph Jones knew that if the troopers sank the *Standard* in the river channel at Melon Bluff, it would effectively block the river and put Montevideo Plantation, a bare two miles upstream, out of the gunboat's reach. The safety of his parents undoubtedly weighed heavily on his mind. The detail of troopers Joseph sent to Melon Bluff soon arrived there with the sad news that they were required to confiscate the vessel and scuttle it in the channel. What a hard moment it must have been to those who had brought the *Standard* through so many difficulties. In the trials of their storm-tossed journey, the crewmen and the ship had blended together as one entity. They had worked together as a team in order to overcome the harsh elements that surrounded them. Now, faced with the reality of quietly losing the *Standard* while it lay at anchor, after it had carried them safely so far and through so much, must have been like losing a true friend. This was not the ending they had anticipated.

Captain Blanch was informed that if he went to the Liberty Independent Troop Headquarters in Riceboro, he would be given a certificate stating that the vessel had been confiscated by the Confederate forces due to wartime emergencies. The ship's owner, Daniel Huntley, would be reimbursed for the value of the vessel by the Confederate government at the war's end, providing the South won the war.

The crewmen packed up their possessions, removed the ship's boat and other equipment that could be salvaged, and went ashore. After all the repair work to prepare the vessel for a return journey, it was now to be consigned to the waters of a shallow coastal Georgia river. The *Standard* was no longer free to fill its sails with wind and rush for the horizon. It was trapped by circumstances beyond the control of those present at Melon Bluff on that afternoon.

Once the crewmen were off the vessel, the troopers boarded and entered the dark and empty hold where they drilled a series of holes in the bottom of the hull. Water immediately began flowing into the ship in cascading fountains, gradually filling the interior. The troopers left the stricken vessel, casting it loose from its moorings, and the group gathered at the landing watched the *Standard* drift slowly, sluggishly away and gradually sink into the river. Soon the waters of the North Newport River were spilling over the decks as the vessel settled onto the muddy channel bottom. In a short time only its masts and upper deck were visible above the surface. The sun sank away behind the western horizon as if lowering the curtain on the *Standard*.

While the *Standard* was being scuttled, at Colonel's Island, Joseph Jones had been trying to instill some fighting spirit in the men collected there. It was ironic that the men of the Liberty Independent Troop did not want to stand and fight the gunboat. That previous November, they had been disgruntled at not being able to participate in the defense of Port Royal at Hilton Head. Now that the opportunity to engage the enemy at their own doorstep was at hand, they seemed to have lost their enthusiasm for a fight. Joseph wrote,

> The men did not seem to comprehend the importance of making a stand at Carrs Neck because they said "the bluff is too low and the gun-boats will rake the woods with shot and shell, especially with grape-shot." I replied that it was absurd to keep in the rear of an enemy and to leave our homes exposed; our place was between danger and our homes. Carrs Neck was the only point of any strategic importance on the river, the Channel running immediately along the well wooded shore, an admirable place for sheltering the men

whilst they picked off the Yankees. If we intended to meet the invader we must expect to run risks and if we were afraid of risking our precious carcasses we had no business to be playing the soldier.

It was said on their side that it was very bad policy to fire on the Yankees, as they would then destroy all the private dwellings within reach of their shot and shell. I replied that it was our duty to resist them on all occasions regardless of private interests. By this means alone could we demonstrate to the North the utter impossibility of conquering the South.[9]

At this moment Joseph must have recalled with an agonizing sense of irony the words he had written to his wife in November, regarding the actions of these same men during the Federal attack at Port Royal. On that November day, as they listened to the sound of the cannons from the distant Federal bombardment, Joseph wrote, "Our troop were for a time wild with excitement and the cry was [']onward to Savannah[!']. Many said that they would be willing to pay thousands, for the chance of being in the battle. One poor young soldier, who was very ill . . . begged and plead[ed] with me to allow him to get up and put on his sword and carbine and said that if the troop went, he

Looking east on the North Newport River, Melon Bluff is seen at the distant left center. Photograph by the author and Lynn Holman.

would follow if he had to crawl on his hands and feet."[10] Where was that spirit now that the enemy was on their very doorstep? Joseph continued his narrative:

> Finally three men [Cpl. Augustus M. McIver, Lt. William C. Stevens, and Lt. George Handley] agreed to accompany me to Carr's Neck. It was dark when we started. The heavens were overcast with clouds and it was impossible to discern your hand before your face. The darkness was so great that we lost our way in the woods and wandered about in the dark for near two hours, but finally reached the lower bluff, not the one where we expected to spend the night, we could here discover nothing. The boat had evidently not passed down so low. We then attempted to reach the most important point and finally succeeded in doing so, after scratching our faces amongst the bushes and nearly losing our eyes.
>
> We tied our horses; and selected for our shelter a large pine-tree just on the waters edge. We spread our blankets on the ground and laid down with the understanding that two should keep watch alternately, with the agreement that we would fire on anything that passed, from a boat, up to [a] Gun-boat. My position was between the Pine-tree and the water with my companions at the back of the tree. My watch came first. In ten minutes my companion as well as the remaining two, were blowing off steam at a terrible rate, running opposition lines to the steam-Gun-boats.[11]

While the *Potomska* remained at anchor in the Crosstides and Joseph Jones and his companions were stumbling through the brush on Carr's Neck, down in Doboy Sound, the *Wamsutta* was being alerted by the arrival of the boat from the *Potomska*. The pilot came aboard and conferred with Lieutenant Commander Semmes about the purpose of Watmough's summons. Semmes then alerted his crew and preparations were made to get underway.[12]

The night passed quietly. At Carr's Neck, Joseph Jones and his companions found guard duty very tiresome, especially after their struggle to reach the bluff where they were posted. Joseph volunteered to take the first watch with one of the others, but he soon realized that this might have been a mistake. He wrote, "This watch was passed alone.

The next found my companions still fast asleep. When aroused they fell asleep again in a few moments and appeared to be perfectly overcome and so I kept watch the entire night. My gun and horseman pistols were lying by my hand, ready for a moments warning. During the still hours of the night, the silence was broken only by the snoring of my companions, save once when I heard the sounds of oars and low voices. The men were aroused, our arms cocked, [but] the sound died away in a few moments. The boat appeared to take another course."[13]

The boat Joseph heard in the river was a small one, manned by three black people who had left from Dorchester and were intent on escaping to the gunboat or the offshore islands. The rowboat had been used to carry provisions to the picket posts located downstream, and the escapees had been fortunate enough to find it loaded with rations that had not been delivered because of the current emergency. The slaves made their way downriver, apparently unaware they had come very near to being caught or fired on by Joseph Jones and his comrades on Carr's Neck. A short time later, as the runaways rounded a bend in the river, they could make out the silhouette of a large ship anchored downstream. They rowed toward it.[14]

The *Potomska* spent the evening quietly anchored in the Crosstides Creek. The big guns were run out, loaded, and ready for action, and the deck watch had been doubled. About 11:00 P.M. the watch sounded the alarm when a small boat was discovered approaching from upstream. The first concern of those aboard was that it might be an enemy attack; however, it was found to contain three black people, likely the same three that Jones had spotted. Watmough allowed them to come aboard, and he questioned them at length. They confirmed that the blockade runner was upstream but also that the river there was narrow and treacherous and that any passage of the gunboat would not be easy.[15]

The three were taken below, and the excitement of the moment slipped away. It was a quiet, overcast night, and there was little to break the silence except the lapping of the water against the sides of the ship, the tread of feet upon the wooden deck, and the creaking of the ship's rigging. Watmough stared through the darkness, across the water and marshes to where he knew the treelines were, and wondered just who might be there, waiting the coming of dawn, just as he was. He knew that tomorrow the *Wamsutta* would arrive, and he felt certain they could easily penetrate the river.

Upstream at that moment, at Montevideo Plantation, there was further sadness for the Reverend and Mrs. Jones. Cinda, another of the sick servants, succumbed to the measles, making four slaves it had taken. Many more remained ill, and the plantation was still a veritable hospital. When would things get better? Could they get any worse?

It was still dark and morning's light many hours away on 26 April when the *Wamsutta* departed Doboy Sound in response to Watmough's summons. The day dawned to a heavy overcast, and the morning darkness seemed to linger longer than usual. About 7:00 A.M. the *Wamsutta* entered Sapelo Sound and proceeded through Johnson Creek to the entrance of the North Newport River, where it anchored to await a tide change. Lookouts could see the *Potomska* several miles to the west across the marsh and water.[16]

The *Potomska* spent a relatively quiet night anchored in Crosstides Creek. Only the arrival of the runaway slaves had disturbed the night. As the gray light of dawn seeped through the overcast, lookouts observed the *Wamsutta* approaching, but when it came to a stop, Watmough thought perhaps they could not see the *Potomska* or had run aground and required assistance. He ordered blank charges fired from one of the 32-pounder cannons in order to mark the ship's position for the *Wamsutta*. Several charges were fired, and then signals flashed across the marshes between the two vessels as communication was established.[17]

Joseph Jones and his companions spent a restless night at Carr's Neck, and when they awoke, they were surprised to find another gunboat about to join the one already in the river. He wrote to his wife, "When morning broke, we saw the long, low, black, three masted craft lying in the same position in which we had left her, but another vessel of the same appearance was in sight. They were firing signal guns and evidently communicating with each other. Two of our companions left us after our slight repast of dry parched coffee, salt beef and biscuits which Mother had placed in my saddle bags. We who remained watched the movement of the Gun-boats, about three miles distant."[18]

At 8:30 A.M. the *Potomska* steamed downstream, again passing Half Moon Bluff, and anchored about 9:00 A.M. below Woodville Plantation to await the *Wamsutta*'s arrival. Noting the *Potomska*'s movement, the *Wamsutta* proceeded up the North Newport River toward the *Potomska*, arriving alongside about 10:00 A.M. While they waited for the tide to change, Semmes and Watmough conferred in order to make plans for a coordinated movement upriver to locate the blockade runner that was the object of the operation.[19]

From the underbrush ashore, others carefully observed the two gunboats while the Confederate forces on Colonel's Island began making plans to attack the vessels if they came upriver again. Word was sent out to all Southern forces in the area to concentrate at Half Moon Bluff as soon as possible. Rain began to sprinkle down from the overcast sky, turning to intermittent showers while the vessels remained at anchor. When the rain let up shortly after noon, the two gunboats raised anchor and proceeded upstream with the *Potomska* in the lead.[20] Once again the Confederate troopers seemed to lose their nerve and allowed the gunboats to pass around Half Moon Bluff unmolested.

One can only wonder what thoughts were going through the minds of the Federal sailors as their vessels leisurely steamed inland. They must have run the full gamut of emotions. The crewmen of the *Potomska* had already been involved in a number of operations along the coast and had faced the uncertain dangers of probing into the inland waterways, where the potential of finding a hostile enemy was always present. For those aboard the *Wamsutta*, the situation was far different. They were new to blockade duty, and their prior service had been limited to liberating some corn from a plantation on Sapelo Island. They had not ventured inland on any of the numerous waterways. This was their first excursion into the interior. Their emotions must have been running much higher than those of the sailors on the *Potomska*. Each sailor was at his post, the big guns manned and sharp eyes alert for any suspicious movements along the tree-lined shores. Regardless of emotions, there must have been a thrill of excitement coursing through each sailor aboard the gunboats as they penetrated deeper into the interior. There certainly was a sense of alarm spreading through the ranks of the Southern soldiers and residents ashore.

During this time Joseph Jones and his companions were still on Carr's Neck, waiting to see if the ships would come upriver toward their position. He wrote, "About [1]2 PM . . . a message arrived from the Captain of the Troop requesting us to hurry down as the boats had repassed Colonel's Island and appeared to be taking a position from which we might fire upon them. We hastened down in time to find that the Troop had again allowed the enemy to pass them unmolested. The boats now ascended the river with great rapidity."[21]

The *Potomska* and *Wamsutta* cruised carefully upstream, leaving the broad, open stretch of marshes and creeks behind them. The lookouts had seen signs of activity ashore, and the sailors were aware that they were under close observation by their enemy. About 1:00 P.M. the gun crews were alerted as the channel narrowed and the shorelines gradually began to close in around the two ships. They were ordered to fire random shells into the trees to keep the Confederates at a respectable distance.[22]

With the sound of cannons reverberating in their ears, the men of the Liberty Independent Troop realized that the two enemy gunboats were going upstream, and no one else was there to defend their homes. Joseph Jones wrote, "The greater portion of [the Troop] now attempted to reach Carr's Neck before they passed. I ran my horse for six miles. We arrived too late however and found that they had just passed Carr's Neck, having thrown shot and shell into the woods."[23]

Jones began to realize that if the gunboats were pursuing the escaped blockade runner, then they did not know it had been sunk and their ascent of the river could serve them no useful purpose. Perhaps the gunboats needed a sign to show them that the runner had been disposed of. His letter continues, "Our next effort was to burn the ship which from the shallowness of the waters, had not been but partially submerged. We were enabled on account of the shallowness of the stream and its many bends and short turns, to run ahead of the boats and fire the vessel."[24]

Captain Blanch and the other crew members of the *Standard* were probably still at Melon Bluff when Jones and the others arrived to apply the torch to the *Standard*'s exposed superstructure. The troopers brought word that the enemy gunboat had been joined by another, that they were both on their way upstream, and only a few miles away at that moment. The soldiers boarded the wreck and set fire to the exposed timbers, and in no time black and gray smoke spiraled upward to mingle with the overcast skies. Sometime after the vessel was burned, Captain Blanch and some crewmen took the *Standard*'s boat and rowed upstream to Riceboro where he was to pick up the promised voucher for reimbursement of the vessel's value.[25]

While this was taking place, the *Potomska* and *Wamsutta* continued upstream unmolested, but the crewmen were fully aware they were under observation from both sides of the river. Sometime after 2:00 P.M., the lookouts sighted a dark smudge on the western horizon, and smoke was noted billowing up from a point several miles upstream. The foliage and distance kept them from determining its source, but Watmough must have deduced that it was probably the blockade runner being consumed by the flames.[26] However, there was also the possibility that the fire was from something else and that the escaped runner was still intact, so he decided to press on.

Clouds overhead threatened rain as the gunboats worked their way upstream. The channel began to narrow, and there was a diminishing amount of maneuvering room because of the falling tide. About 4:00 P.M. the *Wamsutta* grounded, and the *Potomska* dropped downstream to assist. While the men worked to free the gunboat, rain began to fall, slowly at first, but increasing until showers drenched the area.[27]

At Montevideo Plantation, the Jones family had been making preparations to move the sick and evacuate the place if the enemy gunboats came up the river. They had much to do. Joseph wrote in the letter to his wife that after they had burned off the *Standard*'s upper works, he "hurried on in a pouring rain to Montevideo and informed Father and Mother, that the Gun-boats were coming up rapidly and were within four or five miles of the place. At my suggestion they left as soon as possible . . . for Arcadia."[28]

Reverend Jones recorded the affair in a letter he wrote later to Lieutenant Jones.

> Your brother came on to Montevideo, giving his fine horse a ride that tested his bottom fairly, and reached us about half-past 5 or 6 PM. He left the gunboats coming up on the flood [tide], and recommended Mother and myself to take the carriage and Little Sister and go at once to Arcadia and be out of the way in case the enemy should either land or shell the plantation. . . . He had not reached home fifteen minutes to hurry us off before my neighbor

Mr. Calder, managing for Estate J. B. Barnard, sent a boy express to let me know the gunboats were coming up by White's Island not far below the ferry.

Mother had that very day sent to Arcadia three or four loads of household furniture, which she had purposed to do, but sickness and interruptions had prevented till then. And Gilbert and the boys were away! There was energetic movement in the house to get things ready on a short notice. The enemy approaching—a complete surprise! You know your mother's energy. Patience, Flora, Elsie, Tom, Sue and Sam, your brother and myself (after a fashion) were all in motion, Susan and Peggy looking after the baby and her outfit in particular, Cook Kate pushing on tea, the horses and carriage getting (and mule-wagon for baggage), Cato called (and Porter) for instructions, Lymus dispatched as a lookout on the lower [rice] dam, to run immediately and give notice if he saw or heard the gunboats or any boats at all coming up the river. All astir, but no confusion; and much was accomplished in a very short time. A few principal things out of the house and out of the study, and all the rest left! We had been burnt out once [by accidental fire]; might be again. We quietly submitted to the will of God. A hasty cup of tea [for supper]—nothing more.

Just as we were getting into the carriage, Gilbert arrived from Arcadia. The faithful fellow would not let Sam take the [driver's] box; said "he was fresh and wanted nothing to eat and preferred driving his mistress himself; it was pitch dark, and he knew his horses better than anyone else." It was cloudy and very dark; we took a candle in the carriage, which was a great help in driving, and a comfort. The mule-wagon behind us. Your brother stayed to take care of the people.[29]

At this time Captain Blanch and his companions boarded their boat to return downstream to Melon Bluff from Riceboro as daylight slipped away and darkness descended. He had obtained the certificate promised him for the confiscation and destruction of the *Standard,* and in the evening twilight they rowed down the North Newport River, passing by Montevideo Plantation, where Joseph Jones was seeing to the evacuation of the place. Jones recorded,

I posted a black sentinel [Lymus] on the river, with orders to inform me when any boats should make their appearance. Mother and Father had scarcely left before the sentinel informed me that a barge with men was approaching. I could hear the oars. All the people were immediately assembled and started on the road to Arcadia with orders to stop about a half a mile from the house. They obeyed with great cheerfulness. I then examined carefully the premises but could not discover that any landing had been made. The negroes were then recalled to their houses with orders to cook, prepare their clothes and hold themselves in readiness to move at a moments warning. After posting the negro men at different points I took a short nap.[30]

While Joseph Jones was dealing with matters at Montevideo, Reverend Jones and the others were en route to Arcadia Plantation. In his letter to Lieutenant Jones, he recorded, "We had started but a little way when Lymus reported a boat in the river. We had all the lights extinguished, and the people hastened to the brickyard shed, and your brother then went back and reconnoitered. Says it was a boat, but where it went he could not determine; thinks it was a barge sent up on a search and for soundings and then dropped down quietly. . . . When we reached Arcadia the family had retired; but after some knocking we were let in and welcomed, and after supper and worship went tired to bed."[31]

The *Wamsutta* managed to free itself from the mudbank where it had grounded, and the two gunboats continued upstream as daylight began to filter away. About 6:00 P.M. they approached the Sunbury-Riceboro ferry landing near South Hampton, one of Audley M. King's plantations on the south bank. Here they anchored for the night. Since they were a good distance up the river and the shores on both sides held enemy soldiers, the deck watches were doubled, and the big cannons loaded and run out.[32]

In the camp of the Liberty Guards at South Newport, James S. Warnell recorded the day's events in his diary that evening. It had been a quiet day for Warnell, who remained on the fringes of the drama. Having just enlisted with the Liberty Guards, he did not yet have a weapon. However, in view of the present emergency, the Liberty Independent Troop was persuaded to issue its extra weapons to these new recruits. Warnell had been detailed to retrieve the weapons from the troop's armory at McIntosh Station. With an invasion of the county on their hands, the Liberty Independent Troop was happy to have every armed man who could be mustered. Warnell recorded, "Nothing of importance occurred. Pickets saw the enemy from various points. Received intelligence that the enemy was burning Colonel's Island. I and J[ohn] A. Martin went to the Station after arms. A very pleasant trip."[33] The "intelligence that the enemy was burning Colonel's Island" probably derived from the sight of smoke from the burning *Standard* drifting above the trees on the eastern horizon.

A night of uneasiness settled upon the area around the North Newport River. Confederate soldiers and citizens ashore watched and waited at various points along the river while civilians busied themselves in evacuating the threatened area. The two gunboats remained quietly anchored in the river while turmoil unfolded ashore.

The cloudy overcast still hung over Liberty County as the dawn of 27 April approached. It was a spring Sabbath, but the close proximity of the Federal gunboats was not a comforting thought for the local residents. The *Potomska* and *Wamsutta* began threading their way upstream about 5:30 A.M. and soon began to strike sandbars and mudbanks as they proceeded. The *Wamsutta* grounded at 7:00 A.M. but was quickly freed. About 9:00 A.M., as they approached the village of Dorchester, the *Wamsutta* was hailed from the north shore where two black people showed themselves. Semmes gave them permission to come aboard, where he interviewed them. He noted in his report that they "informed us that the smoke observed by us at 2 PM the previous day was the burning of the brig, she having been stripped, scuttled, and fired at that time."[34]

This must have been welcome news to the sailors, for the object of their mission had been accomplished for them. After a short conference between Watmough and Semmes, it was agreed to press on upriver while the channel permitted their passage. A short distance upstream, they passed the landing at J. B. Barnard's plantation on the south bank of the river, and just beyond that the *Potomska* grounded. The *Wamsutta* anchored while the *Potomska* worked to free itself. The two vessels were barely a mile below Melon Bluff, hidden from view by a thin peninsula of land around which the river flowed. Semmes recorded in his report, "Having gone thus far . . . a point was reached [where the *Potomska* grounded] where the river became so very narrow, with a still narrower channel, that we deemed in imprudent to go any farther."[35]

The men had no idea how close they had come to the wreck of the *Standard*. If they had, perhaps they would have tried to go further up or would have sent boats ahead, but with the *Potomska* grounded in the channel, no forward progress could be made. They could only await the tide change to free the vessel and then use the ebb tide to carry them back down the river.

Long before dawn, Joseph Jones had been hard at work at Montevideo Plantation. After a short nap, he saw to the packing up and evacuating of everything that could be saved from the place. He wrote to his wife that when he awoke and returned to work, he "packed and buried Mother's crockery and glassware, ordered the ox and mule carts, packed them with the bedding and most valuable furniture and sent them to Arcadia together with the women and children. I kept a strict watch myself over the river, determined to fire into any barges which might ascend. I dispatched an express to Arcadia for all the ox-carts. Aunt Susan very kindly sent her Carts also. I was determined that if the Yankees came up, they should have a barren victory. I had also determined to fire the corn and cotton rather than to let it fall into their hands."[36]

Reverend Jones, at Arcadia Plantation, recorded in the letter to his oldest son,

> Your dear brother was up on the watch all night. Gilbert went back to him, and with all the servants packing all night, about daylight the oxcarts were packed with furniture and household matters of every kind and sent off for Arcadia. Meanwhile the carts from Arcadia and Lambert [plantations] were dispatched. And Sabbath (as it was) we had a stream of carts and wagons running all day between the two places; and by sundown your brother had nearly everything moved out of the house, and nearly all the women and children and some of the sick men moved over also. He says he never saw servants more attentive or take a greater interest in the removal and effort to keep clear of the enemy.[37]

On that same morning of 27 April, the Liberty Guards sent out a detachment of men that included James Warnell. They were to assist in repelling the invasion of the North Newport River and were hopeful of locating a position on the south bank from which they could fire on the enemy gunboats. James recorded, "Left camp with a detachment under Lieuts. [A. B.] Daniel and [John E.] Zoucks, 12 privates [and] 1 non-commissioned officer. The whole party of 13 went to Barnard's place where we met Mrs. Calder who informed us that the enemy was at the Landing. She made a negro pilot us to that point before we found the position of the Federals. They commenced shelling us which caused considerable excitement. I and Lieut. Daniel and White went under cover of the bushes and had a tolerably fair view of the Yankee's boats, 2 in number. We did not fire on them because we thought [it] best to get all the boys there and give them a deck raking. Before our force got to us we was discovered by the Seamen who ran into their boat as quick as rats to their holes."[38]

The two gunboats had been anchored off Barnard's Landing throughout the morning, and lookouts were quick to notice the increased activity in the underbrush on the south shore. They wasted no time in firing a few shells into the brush to keep the curious at a respectable distance, for the ships were well within carbine range.[39]

Upstream at Melon Bluff, Captain Blanch and the crew of the *Standard* were preparing to evacuate the area when they were startled by the sound of cannons just downstream from their location. It was all the incentive they needed to leave. They piled their belongings into the *Standard*'s boat, climbed in, and pushed off from the landing. Several men took their places at the oars, and with a slack tide they began pulling upstream, bound for Riceboro.

Just upstream at Montevideo Plantation, Joseph Jones was packing up the last of the furniture. In a letter he wrote to his wife, he continued,

> Every article of furniture, all the books, etc. were made ready to start for Arcadia, when a body of armed citizens rode up and requested me to show them the way to the Gun-boats. I immediately went with them. We found the Gun-boats at Mr. Barnard's. . . . Whilst we were viewing one boat which lay so as to completely command the roads, a barge was seen advancing up river, towards Montevideo. It was determined that we should return and attack this [barge] as we could do nothing at all against one Gun-boat which was out of reach

The Montevideo boat landing as seen today, looking north. The North Newport River is seen just beyond. This landing, dug from the marsh by slave labor, was where Joseph hailed the crewmen of the Standard *as they passed upstream, bound for Riceboro, on that afternoon of 27 April 1862. Photograph by the author and Lynn Holman.*

of our guns. When we arrived at Montevideo we heard the boat coming up and took our positions. I hurried off the negroes and carts, knowing that if this was the enemy's boat, it [the landing] would be attended with the probable destruction of the house. I took my stand on the landing in front of the house. As soon as the boat was in gun shot [range] I hailed it and found that it was a boat from the burnt ship and was consequently filled with friendly sailors.[40]

The residents of Liberty County were very religious people, and it being a Sunday, not even Yankee gunboats could deter them from attending services at Midway Church, some ten miles from the gunboats. However, even in the sanctity of the Lord's house, they were uneasy. Word that the enemy was coming upriver in barges spread quickly. The Reverend Jones, at Arcadia Plantation, received the news and determined to assist in the defense of his home in any way possible. He wrote to his oldest son:

Your mother and Aunt Susan and Cousins Lyman and Laura[41] went to church, but I was too inactive to go and remained [at Arcadia] with the children. But on the report of the boys with the oxcarts that the

Time to Pay the Piper

enemy were coming up in open barges, that your brother had a detachment of men at Montevideo . . . and others had gone over to Mr. Barnard's and were preparing to attack them, I felt I must go, and ordered the buggy. And your aunt got me a little relish, having taken but one sermon with Mother. And putting your little revolver on the seat by me, refusing to let Mother go with me as she desired to do, I drove off, meeting carriages on the road returning from church. At [Riceboro] I learned that the barges proved to be the yawl of the Nova Scotia vessel coming up to the Boro with the seamen. But the gunboats were lying at the ferry, had not gone up to Busby's landing, and had fired a shell or two at Captain Hughes' men near Mr. J. B. Barnard'[s] settlement, but did no one any damage. Part of Captain Hughes' company [Liberty Guards] had come over to aide from their encampment at South Newport.[42]

It is not known for certain what Captain Blanch and the crewmen of the *Standard* did when they reached Riceboro. They may have sold the ship's boat to someone in Riceboro as they would have had no further need for it. From Riceboro they could have gone to McIntosh Station, where transportation to Savannah or Darien could be obtained. At that time several steamers were lying far up the Altamaha River, waiting for the chance to slip out through the blockade. They might be in need of the services of experienced seamen and a coastal river pilot.

After his near brush with the crewmen of the *Standard* at Montevideo landing, Joseph Jones left his companions at the house and proceeded to ride along the shoreline to reconnoiter the river. In skirting a swampy area his horse wandered into a bog that quickly trapped both horse and rider. Joseph managed to get out and, after much trouble, extricated his horse as well. Wet and uncomfortable, he returned to Montevideo, where he provided quite a sight to his friends who waited there.[43]

Shortly after noon, the tide turned, and the *Potomska* worked free of the sandbar where it had grounded. Once freed, the *Potomska* joined the *Wamsutta*, and the two gunboats let the falling tide carry them downstream. Lieutenant Commander Semmes recorded that "both vessels started down on the ebb [tide], backing or going head first, as the tide happened to take them. We took the bottom so often that we began to expect it at every bend."[44]

Both vessels retired downstream, but they were to encounter far more resistance on their retreat than to their initial incursion. Back at Barnard's Landing, James Warnell and his comrades were just discovering that the enemy gunboats had slipped away. He recorded,

After staying in the woods near the landing for some two hours we went out to the house when we met several of the Independent Troop. In a short time we found that [the] boats had made down the river. Our next and only chance was King's Landing, 5 miles distance. We was ordered to that point in double quick and instead of double quick we went at triple quick but got there too late. But we dismounted and got as near as possible which was out of range of our rifles. Four of us, Grace [Grice], [W. H.] Duke and the Commissary ran down some mile and a half to a point which was in range where we gave them several rounds which appeared to give them some uneasiness. After we opened fire on them [they] raised steam and sail and went off in a hurry. We come back to where we left our horses and the boys was all gone but left a boy to take care of our horses and direct us to go to Mr. [Audley] King's house.[45]

Joseph Jones and his comrades remained at Montevideo Plantation to await further developments. A short time later Reverend Jones arrived on the scene in his buggy, having traveled from Arcadia to aid in the defense of the plantation. In the letter to his oldest son, he wrote,

Riding up to Montevideo house, the scene was lovely: Horses hitched about, others grazing with their saddles on, and little groups of soldiers and men here and there, and the stoop full of them. They all gave me a hearty welcome. . . .

"But where is Joe?"

"Oh, the Doctor! We have all prescribed him to go and lie down and rest, for he has been up the whole of two nights, had been riding to and fro all day watching for the enemy in the river."

Not long after, he appeared at the upstairs window in his shirt sleeves, looking like a man just out of a nap. He came down in wet stockings: his boots drying. Had ridden, in reconnoitering along the swamp, into a spring bog which came up to his knees on horseback almost to the crupper of his saddle. The horse by great exertions got out.

Mr. Edgar Way now arrived and reported that the gunboats had left the ferry and were steaming down to Colonel's Island, where a part of the troop had gone to fire upon them on their way down.[46]

Lt. William A. Fleming of the Liberty Independent Troop wrote in his memoirs, "In the mean time the signal agreed upon, had been heard, and all the old and retiring members [of the Troop] had gathered together, as a band of brothers, to resist the invaders, and posted themselves on the Half Moon Bluff."[47]

Reverend Jones's narrative continued: "About the time they would reach the Island we heard their cannon. . . . Nearly all [the men gathered at Montevideo] now started for the Island. Two returned to sick families at Walthourville, leaving Mr. Thomas W. Fleming, Rev. D. L. Buttolph [pastor of the Midway Church] (who came on after church), Robert [Mallard], Joe and myself."[48]

The Federal sailors aboard the gunboats were probably glad to be descending the river and returning to the open space of the marshes, waterways, and offshore islands. The river channel was too confining, and the enemy soldiers ashore had been a nuisance, taking potshots at them. It took the gunboats a little over four hours to traverse the river downstream because of difficulties with sandbars and mudbanks. The green foliage of the shorelines gradually withdrew, and eventually the river began to widen, allowing for easier movement. When the broad expanse of water and marsh came into view, it seemed as if they would make their return to the open seas without further interference from the Confederate soldiers ashore.

The *Wamsutta* and the *Potomska* picked their way downstream, with the *Wamsutta* in the lead. Once past Carr's Neck, they proceeded toward Colonel's Island and Half Moon Bluff, the last point from which the Confederates might oppose their passage. The sailors aboard both ships had been at their posts all afternoon, but none dared to relax now as each passing moment brought them closer to Half Moon. Aboard the *Wamsutta* the guncrew of the 20-pounder Parrott rifle on the forward-deck pivot remained alert. Like most of the *Wamsutta's* crew, these men were all newly enlisted, and this was their first taste of active service on the blockade.

As the *Wamsutta* approached the western end of Half Moon Bluff, Semmes ordered the rifled pivot gun and one of the forward 32-pounders each to fire into the woods ahead to clear out anyone who might be there. The 20-pounder Parrott rifle sent a shell whistling into the woods, followed closely after by a stand of grapeshot from one of the 32-pounders. The thunderous reports echoed across the marshes and through the trees as the smell of burned black powder drifted over the deck of the *Wamsutta*.[49]

Along the brush-covered banks of Half Moon Bluff, the citizens and troopers of the Liberty Independent Troop were bringing their weapons to bear, anxiously fingering the triggers, counting the seconds as the steamers closed the distance from the western end of the bluff. At last the long-awaited moment had arrived when the Liberty Independent Troop would be able to close with their enemy and demonstrate their resistance to being ruled by force. Their long-sought baptism of fire was at hand. Lieutenant Fleming, who was on the bluff at that moment, recalled in later years, "The boats descended peaceably and quietly until they arrived opposite the west end of the Bluff, when the firing began with Sharps' Carbines."[50]

When the first volley of gunfire burst from the covering foliage along the bluff, Quartermaster George Boswell and Seaman James Brown, members of the *Wamsutta's* Parrott rifle guncrew, fell mortally wounded. Brown fell with a bullet in the abdomen, while Boswell had been struck by a bullet in his upper left abdomen that coursed downward, exiting out his lower right hip. They both bled profusely, and Boswell vomited considerably until taken below decks.[51]

Semmes wrote in his report of this action that "The rebels opened a heavy fire upon us, at a distance of from 20 to 30 yards, with rifles. This vessel [the *Wamsutta*] was ahead and grounded in the bend when under this fire. We replied to their fire with shells, grape, and canister."[52] Fleming recalled that the shot, shell, and canister "did no damage, on account of the elevation of the bluff."[53]

With the *Wamsutta* grounded in the channel, the Federal sailors on board had difficulty keeping up their return fire under the leaden hail of bullets. The *Potomska* was still free to maneuver and quickly brought its broadsides to bear, firing of shells and grapeshot into the foliage that covered the bluff and concealed the Confederates. Semmes recorded in his report, "Fortunately the <u>Potomska</u> could bring her battery to bear when our guns could not be used. At one point our starboard battery was used to assist the <u>Potomska</u>. The <u>Potomska</u>'s fire was well directed and of great assistance to us. She had no casualties."[54]

The *Wamsutta*'s use of its starboard guns illustrates how close to the bluff the ship was. The port guns, facing the bluff, could not be elevated to fire over the bluff. The starboard guns, facing away from the bluff, had to be brought around and fired across the deck of the vessel in order to shoot over the bluff at the Confederates.

With the *Wamsutta* grounded under a raking fire and the *Potomska* unable to pass downstream, things could have been very uncomfortable for the two steamers. Fortunately the *Wamsutta* was able to free itself, and the two gunboats steamed off at full speed trying to pass the bluff as quickly as possible. The Confederate troopers continued to move along the bluff, keeping pace with the vessels as they passed and pouring a rapid volume of fire upon them. Joseph Jones recorded that "As [the vessels] passed Woodville they fired shot and shell through Mrs.

View of Half Moon Bluff as seen today, looking west. Photograph by the author.

Looking downstream from Half Moon Bluff toward Sapelo Sound. The King Plantation of Woodville was located on the bank at the distant left. Photograph by the author.

King's house and out-buildings."[55] Lieutenant Fleming recalled that the gunboats passed "as rapidly as they could be propelled by steam, our men continuing their fire until they were out of range for their rifles."[56]

The *Wamsutta* and *Potomska* finally steamed away from the Confederate soldiers on Colonel's Island, much to the relief of those on board. The open expanse of marshes and the broad channel of the lower North Newport River must have been a welcome sight to the sailors. On the *Wamsutta*, Semmes recorded that "The negroes [who came in after the event] put the rebel force at about 100. The rapidity of their fire went to show that to be nearly correct. . . . Our port side bore pretty good evidence of the enemy's fire, which commenced at 5:10 and ended at 6:20 [P.M.]."[57]

The *Potomska* fired twenty-five rounds from her big guns in support of the grounded *Wamsutta*, but, for the amount of lead being fired at the two gunboats in the hour-long skirmish, casualties aboard the vessels were surprisingly light. The *Potomska* sustained no casualties, and aboard the *Wamsutta* only Boswell and Brown had been wounded, but their wounds were mortal. They were treated with a mixture of opium, whiskey, and brandy administered every ten minutes, but each draught was quickly vomited up. Bandages and compresses were applied to their wounds, and they were made as comfortable as possible, but there was little hope.[58]

Boswell and Brown had enlisted in the navy only two months before and had joined the *Wamsutta*'s crew at the Philadelphia Navy Yard. Seaman James Brown was a twenty-nine-year-old native of Waicham, Massachusetts; and Quartermaster George Boswell was a thirty-eight-year-old native of Philadelphia. Boswell was married and had left a wife of eight years at home when he joined the navy and went off to fight the war. Now the war, the cause for which they fought, was demanding the ultimate sacrifice of these two men.[59]

While events unfolded at Half Moon Bluff, Reverend Jones, his son Joseph, and the others remaining at Montevideo heard the rumble of the cannons downstream. Joseph Jones wrote to his wife that "We heard the reports of cannon which grew worse and then faint and finally ceased."[60] Reverend Jones wrote in a letter to Lieutenant Jones that "The firing was continuous, but not very rapid, for half an hour or three-quarters, upon which we concluded [that] our men had fired upon them and they had [probably] shelled the woods and Woodville [Mrs. King's] and Maxwell settlements [on the Island]. . . . The enemy being gone, there was no need of any further guard at this point; and about sundown the three ministers and the planter [Reverend Jones] and the doctor [Joseph] retired in single file—the planter in the lead—to our homes."[61]

James Warnell and his three companions from the Liberty Guards spent the late afternoon traveling to meet up with the rest of their detachment at South Hampton Plantation, Audley King's house, located on the south bank of the North Newport River. He recorded in his diary that they "arrived there and found all hands eating supper which we joined them in. While eating [we] heard the Independent Troop and gun boats fighting at Colonel's Island."[62]

The gunboats retired downstream in the evening twilight. Aboard the *Wamsutta* at 7:15 P.M., Quartermaster Boswell died of his wounds, but Seaman Brown lingered. The ships came to anchor about 7:45 P.M. in the mouth of the North Newport River near Johnson Creek.[63]

With darkness settling across the land and the gunboats with their imminent threat of invasion finally removed from the river, Reverend

Jones, Joseph, and their companions gladly retired to their homes. Reverend Jones wrote, "Robert [Mallard] and Joe came home with Brother Buttolph to Arcadia. Supper; family worship . . . then bed. Such a Sabbath I never spent before—and wish to spend none other like it."[64] Quiet returned to Liberty County once again. Aboard the *Wamsutta,* at 10:35 P.M. Seaman Brown died of his wounds.[65]

⋯⇒ SIX ⇐⋯

Aftermath

T he *Potomska* and *Wamsutta* remained anchored near the mouth of the North Newport River throughout the night. In the predawn darkness of 28 April 1862, Lieutenant Commander Watmough sent the *Potomska*'s pilot to the *Wamsutta* to guide it back to Doboy Sound. The gunboats moved to Sapelo Sound about 5:00 A.M. and remained there until the gray light of dawn penetrated the overcast. The *Wamsutta* departed shortly after 8:30 A.M., leaving the *Potomska* in Sapelo Sound. The *Wamsutta* proceeded down the inland passage behind Sapelo Island until the falling tide forced it to anchor. While waiting, a landing party went ashore to La Chatlet Plantation on the northwest end of Sapelo Island, where they obtained lumber to build coffins.[1]

Joseph Jones rose early and returned to Montevideo to finish removing the goods and people remaining there. While there, he wrote a letter to his wife to relate the details of the past few days' events. Regarding the situation at Montevideo he wrote, "The house at Montevideo is now completely dismantled. . . . Notwithstanding the great fatigue, the excitement sustained me and I was enabled to endure it without any discomfort. Mother and Father and Little Ruth are still at Arcadia. I do not think that the Gun=boats will make another trip. I am very glad that I was here to render this assistance to Mother and Father. Poor Father is so feeble that it would have been absolutely impossible for him to have directed the move. My greatest regret is that it was done chiefly on the Sabbath. . . . Father regretted exceedingly that he was unable to show his resistance to these infamous Pirates. . . . I am rejoiced that I did not leave the County until this was all over. The Troop sustained its old reputation by firing upon the Yankees. All is now quiet."[2]

At Arcadia Plantation Reverend and Mrs. Jones spent a day of relative relaxation after the anxiety and tensions of the past few days. Reverend Jones wrote to Lieutenant Jones to relate the excitement of recent events:

All the [Black] women have been sent back from Arcadia this morning except those with little children and the little children. We are now hauling and storing the corn from Montevideo in part of the Arcadia cornhouse, and may remove the cotton also. Arcadia is less exposed, we think, than Montevideo. I regret our inability last fall to remove all our people back from the seaboard. We should have been saved much anxiety, and we know not yet what loss. . . .

I do not know what we should have done without your brother. He has done everything for us he could, and I feel that he has been the means of saving the lives of several of the servants in our recent illnesses. All, thanks to divine mercy, are better. . . .

We have had a hospital at Montevideo for four full weeks. Wally died on the 4th, Joe on the 16th, Old Niger on the 24th, and—last —Cinda on the 25th. . . . Several have been extremely ill. The last case . . . now better. Three of the Savannah men yet not at work: convalescing. Four deaths and an entire evacuation of house and home for fear of the enemy in four weeks! These are some of the sad changes of life—and all from this unnatural and cruel war. What remains we know not.[3]

By sunset of 28 April, the *Wamsutta* was safely anchored off Doboy Island once again, and the *Potomska*'s pilot was sent off to return to that vessel. At 7:15 P.M. a cutter was lowered from the *Wamsutta* with a detail of six men who were sent ashore on Doboy Island to dig two graves.

At 8:30 P.M., with a clear night sky above them, the two coffins were taken ashore and a brief service held over the remains of Brown and Boswell. Four days later, on 2 May, their clothing was auctioned off among the crew, the proceeds going to the families of Brown and

Boswell. On the morning of 11 June, twenty men from the *Wamsutta* went ashore on Doboy Island and placed headboards and constructed a picket fence around the graves.[4]

Watmough and Semmes submitted written reports that were forwarded through the chain of command. Admiral Du Pont stated in his report to the secretary of the navy that the loss to the Confederates "as reported by contrabands who came in shortly after, was 16 killed and 43 wounded."[5] This was more wishful thinking than fact, for the soldiers and citizens who rallied to the defense of their homes actually suffered no recorded casualties. Reverend Jones wrote, "They fired their guns, but the balls and shells went over our men, and we had nobody hurt."[6]

Word of the *Standard*'s demise eventually made its way back to Halifax, Nova Scotia. The *Halifax Evening Express* newspaper of 20 June 1862 published the following notice:

> Accounts were received here yesterday by the R.M.S. [Royal Mail Ship] <u>Delta</u> from St. Thomas, Bermuda, of the safe arrival hence of the brigt. <u>Standard</u> at a point in Florida [sic], having succeeded in safely running the blockade of the southern ports. The <u>Standard</u> was forty-eight days out before she succeeded in getting into port. The Captain sold his cargo and after discharging it burned the vessel by requisition of the Confederates, in order that she should not fall into the hands of the Federals. The Confederate authorities gave the Captain of the <u>Standard</u> a certificate to that effect, and also that when the existing difficulties are settled between the North and South, the latter will pay for the vessel.[7]

It is probable that some of the *Standard*'s crew had safely run the blockade out of Georgia and arrived in St. Thomas, bringing the news of the *Standard*'s fate. Tom Hernandez piloted the steamer *Agnes* out of Doboy Sound in late May or early June 1862, and he would have been in the St. Thomas area about the time the RMS *Delta* was there. Perhaps James Dickson was also there with Hernandez.

At the Chatham Artillery camp near Savannah, Lt. Charles Jones C. Jr. must have read and reread the letter his father sent him describing the affair. Jones was sorry that he had not been able to participate in some way, and on 30 April he wrote to his father:

I cannot sufficiently thank you for your minute, graphic and deeply interesting letter of the 28th inst., this afternoon received. It grieves me deeply to know that home—a place so peculiarly consecrated to peace, quiet, religion, hospitality, and true happiness, the abode of my honored and beloved parents and of my precious little daughter —should have been so ruthlessly disturbed in its security and calm repose by the near approach of those lawless bands of robbers and freebooters who are now infesting our coast. . . . I presume the immediate object in the contemplation of the enemy in coming up the river was the destruction of the vessel at Busby's landing. Of the fact of the vessel having passed up the river I imagine the blockading fleet had due notice, as they seem to be apprised of almost everything which transpires along our coast. I do not think the gunboats will return.

The burning of the vessel and the alacrity with which all armed upon the first note of alarm are most praiseworthy. Do offer my congratulations to [brother Joseph] for his energy and most valuable services. I am sorry that he did not enjoy the opportunity of discharging at least both barrels well loaded with buckshot from Grandfather's genuine "Mortimer". . . full in the face, at easy range of the nefarious rascals. I would have given a great deal to have had a section of our battery at Half Moon and treated the Lincolnites to a dose of shell and canister. A light battery is very effective under such circumstances.

It is a most unfortunate circumstance when the holy quiet of the Sabbath is disturbed by the rude alarms of war; but the obligations of national defense and of the protection of our homes and lives and property from the attacks of an invading foe are as sacred on that as on any other day. . . .

I could not but contrast in my mind the appearance of the river disturbed by the Lincoln gunboats—the trees marred by iron missiles, and the still air rent by the noise of cannon and of firearms and filled with the strange smell of battle. . . . Half Moon Bluff has now become somewhat historical. I hope that the enemy suffered loss and harm in the skirmish, in order that they may be deterred from adventuring a second time.[8]

Lieutenant Jones's hope—that the gunboats might be deterred from venturing into the inland waterways again—proved to be in vain. The ever-increasing numbers of blockaders meant they would continue to push into the inland waterways when necessary, and with the cordon established in the entrances to the sounds in April 1862, the coast was all but closed down. With so many gunboats prowling about, Southern homes within reach of the waterways were considered fair game and were often visited by landing parties sent ashore from the blockaders. The incursion into the North Newport River would not prove to be an isolated incident on Georgia's coast. The Federal gunboats would strike again.

In November 1862 the *Potomska* and *Darlington* ascended the Sapelo River, landed Federal troops at Mallow Plantation, and took away all the slaves. Upstream the troops landed at several points, and other plantations were shelled and set on fire while U.S. troops skirmished with Confederate cavalry. In June 1863 black troops landed from U.S. gunboats at Darien, and the town was looted and burned. As salt became scarce, salting operations grew along the coast to distill the salt from seawater. These quickly became targets of Federal naval operations, and the gunboats destroyed many of them; troops made numerous landings in search of them.

In August 1864 a detachment of U.S. sailors and marines ascended the South Newport River to surprise and capture an entire company of South Carolina cavalry encamped at the South Newport campground. That same month other sailors and marines landed from the Sapelo River and surprised and captured a public meeting being held at the McIntosh County Court House to raise a militia company. The prisoners were marched southward along the coastal highway to Darien, where they rendezvoused with gunboats that took them off.

Throughout the remaining years of the war, the blockade was an ever-tightening thing. It grew in strength and quality of ships, and, in the later years of the war, was especially effective on the Georgia coast. Since the Federal vessels were not afraid to steam up deep-water rivers in search of blockade runners, very few ports offered a safe haven. Blockade running continued up to the very last days of the war and successful runs were still made on the Georgia coast in spite of the vigilant blockade.

The arrival of the *Standard* and the subsequent invasion of the North Newport River by the gunboats were events that the residents along that river would not soon forget, and it had a great impact on them and their perceptions of the war. This was the first time they had been forced to see the face of the war from the comfort of their homes, and they began to realize just what it meant to be living practically on the front lines, within easy reach of a sudden attack by an enemy who was never more than a few miles away. When the *Potomska* and *Darlington* ascended the Sapelo River in November 1862, they landed troops who confiscated slaves, skirmished with the local defense forces, burned a few buildings, and slipped away back out to sea aboard their gunboats. All of this happened only about fifteen miles south of Montevideo Plantation, and it called forth vivid memories for the residents of Liberty County of the invasion of their own river that spring. The incursion into the North Newport River was a key event for the residents, and it shaped many of their thoughts and concepts of the war on the coast, until Sherman's army brought the dawning of a new era of warfare.

The citizens and soldiers vowed never to be caught unprepared again. That December while at Montevideo to oversee sugarcane-grinding operations, Reverend Jones wrote his aunt, Eliza Robarts, on 13 December 1862 that "The home guard (of old men and boys) will meet next week to dig rifle pits below the ferry and at Half Moon on the Island and perhaps Carr's Neck and Melon Bluff (Mr. Busby's place) in case the vessels should come up as they did last spring."[9]

Busby closed his home at Melon Bluff that fall and moved further inland to Taylor's Creek. The strain of having enemy gunboats advance up the river to within a mile of his landing, intent on coming up to it, was more than the seventy-five-year-old gentleman wished to contend with. The possibility of a reoccurrence of the incident was too frightening, so Busby removed himself and family from the danger. He died at Taylor's Creek that winter and was buried at Midway Cemetery.[10]

Perhaps it was because of the narrowness of the North Newport or maybe because no more blockade runners sought refuge there, but Federal gunboats never intruded very far into Liberty County's inland waterways again. Liberty County and its residents were left relatively undisturbed throughout the remainder of the war though sharp eyes were always kept to the east, where the enemy lay in sight every day. However, the real war came rumbling up to Liberty County's doorstep in December 1864 with the arrival of General Sherman's army, which approached from the west. Its visit would make the invasion of the North Newport River look like a Sunday outing.

The Reverend and Mrs. Jones never again resided at their beloved Montevideo Plantation for any length of time after April 1862. The plantation continued to operate in their absence under the supervision of their neighbor, James R. Calder, and they occasionally returned for short visits and to conduct business there, but after April 1862 it was felt that living on the river was too dangerous. Reverend and Mrs. Jones stayed at Arcadia until 19 May 1862, when they returned to Montevideo for one week. Reverend Jones wrote to Lieutenant Jones from there on 22 May: "We removed home on Monday after a delightful visit at Arcadia of three weeks. . . . The plantation is still a hospital. Near twenty cases of sickness, all connected with the measles."[11] Eventually the epidemic would subside, but not before taking four servants from them.

On 26 May 1862 Reverend and Mrs. Jones journeyed to Walthourville to reside with their daughter and son-in-law, the Reverend Robert Q. Mallard, who was pastor of the Walthourville Church. They remained there throughout the summer and fall of 1862 and on 1 December 1862 returned to Arcadia, where they stayed until Reverend Jones died there on 16 March 1863. He was buried in Midway Cemetery. It was fortunate that he did not live to see what eventually became of his beloved home.[12]

After her husband's death Mary Jones lived with her daughter in Walthourville but continued to operate Montevideo and Arcadia plantations. On the approach of Sherman's forces in December 1864, she, her daughter, and several friends fled to Montevideo for refuge, which was felt to be more isolated from the main roads and less likely to be molested by Federal troops. Thus they came full circle. Back in April 1862 they had fled Montevideo because it was seen as dangerous and too exposed to the possibility of naval landing parties coming from the river. Two and a half years later, they returned to Montevideo to take refuge from another threat from a different direction, that of

General Sherman. In the rush of events that transpired after Sherman's arrival on the coast, the memories of those April days in 1862 paled by comparison.

Throughout December 1864 and January 1865, the family was subjected to almost daily visits from Federal soldiers from Sherman's army, foraging for food and plunder. The soldiers tore up the houses, took the food, the livestock, and the belongings of everyone, black or white. They burned homes, barns, and outbuildings and tore up the railroad through the entire county. By February 1865 Liberty County was a wasteland of broken homes and broken dreams. Food was scarce, starvation common, and lawless bands of former slaves began harassing the residents. Many people left their homes and fled to safer regions, some never to return.[13]

Mary Jones and her daughter fled Liberty County in late March 1865, going to stay with relatives in Baker County in southwest Georgia. She returned to Montevideo in October 1865 with plans to maintain the three Jones plantations in Liberty County. However, she found that Maybank, their home on Colonel's Island, had been burned in April 1865 by marauding gangs of black people, and Arcadia had almost forcibly been taken from her by the many freed slaves who took up residence there and refused to leave when asked to do so.[14]

Mary Jones struggled on at Montevideo, with her family scattered in all directions. Charles C. Jones Jr. was in New York practicing law, Joseph was in Nashville teaching, and her daughter (Mrs. Mallard) and her family had moved to New Orleans, where Reverend Mallard accepted a position as pastor of a church. Mary Jones left Montevideo and Liberty County in January 1868, going to live with her daughter's family in New Orleans. She died there on 23 April 1869 and was buried in LaFayette Cemetery.[15]

Lt. Charles C. Jones Jr. remained in the Confederate service throughout the war. On 14 October 1862 he was appointed lieutenant colonel of artillery and assigned duty as chief of artillery for the state of Georgia. He was the chief of artillery for Confederate forces during the siege of Savannah in December 1864.[16] Following the war, he continued in law practice in New York City until 1877, when he returned to Georgia and settled at Montrose, his home in Summerville, near Augusta. There he practiced law and wrote many historical works. He married for a second time in October 1863 and died in Augusta on 19 July 1893. He was buried in the Summerville Cemetery.[17]

Joseph Jones remained in the Confederate Army throughout the war, conducting medical research in Confederate camps and among U.S. prisoners in various prison camps throughout the South. After the war he and his wife moved to Tennessee, where he taught at the Medical College of Nashville (1866–68). He then moved to New Orleans, where he taught at the University of Louisiana (1868–94) and was surgeon general of the United Confederate Veterans (1889–96). He wrote many medical works and is best known for his contributions to that science. His wife Caroline died in 1868, leaving him with four children. He later married the daughter of Confederate general Leonidas Polk in 1871, and they had three children. He died in New Orleans on 17 February 1896 and is buried in LaFayette Cemetery.[18]

The *Potomska* blockaded Sapelo Sound and St. Catherine's Sound through June 1863 and continued to serve on the southeast coast throughout the war. It was the first vessel fired on by Fort McAllister on the Ogeechee River in July 1862. It was refitted at Northern navy yards twice during the war and, through its entire service, captured only one blockade runner. On 16 June 1865 the *Potomska* was decommissioned at the Philadelphia Navy Yard and sold at public auction on 30 August 1865 for seventy-one hundred dollars.[19]

Pendleton G. Watmough left the *Potomska* in August 1862 to take command of the USS *Memphis.* In September 1862 he married Mary M. Merwin, a granddaughter of an Ohio governor, at Rockport, Ohio. In May 1863 he left the *Memphis,* which had been damaged by Confederate ironclads off Charleston, and was ordered to the Philadelphia Navy Yard for ordnance duty, where he stayed until November 1863, when he took command of the USS *Kansas.* He participated in the blockade off Wilmington, North Carolina, where the *Kansas* captured several blockade runners.[20]

In the spring of 1865 the *Kansas* was ordered to the James River, where it participated in the final bombardment of the Confederate river batteries prior to the evacuation of Richmond. In May 1865 he returned to Philadelphia Navy Yard for ordnance duty, and he resigned his commission in July 1865. In 1869 he was appointed collector of customs at Cleveland, Ohio, by President Grant, and he was reappointed in 1873. The Watmoughs had four children, and in 1889 the family returned to Philadelphia, where Watmough retired to Maple Lawn at Chestnut Hill. At the age of eighty-three, he quietly passed away at the Presbyterian Hospital, on 20 April 1911 following a long illness.[21]

The *Wamsutta* remained on blockade duty at Doboy Sound until July 1862, when it was sent north for the repair of a broken air pump. During its service the *Wamsutta* captured one blockade runner and was responsible for the destruction of two others. It was eventually reassigned to another squadron. On 29 June 1865 the *Wamsutta* was decommissioned at Portsmouth, New Hampshire, Navy Yard and sold at public auction on 20 July 1865 for $14,500.[22]

Alexander A. Semmes left the *Wamsutta* in October 1862 to command the USS *Tahoma*. He went on to serve with the East Gulf Blockading Squadron in command of several vessels, was responsible for the capture of several blockade runners, and participated in raids on Tampa, Florida. He served with the Southeast Blockading Squadron again off Charleston. On 9 February 1864 he married Mary M. Dorsey at Baltimore, Maryland. By the war's end he was commanding the ironclad USS *Lehigh,* a monitor-class vessel built in April 1863, serving in the James River near Richmond, Virginia.[23]

In March 1865 he was ordered to the Philadelphia Navy Yard. When the war ended, he remained in the navy, serving in the East Indies, off China, and in Africa before being suspended for three years in January 1872 as a result of a general court-martial. The reasons for this are unknown. In December 1872 the court-martial sentence was dropped, and he was ordered in January 1873 to the U.S. Navy Yard at Pensacola, Florida. In 1883 he was ordered to take command of the Washington, D.C., Navy Yard.[24]

On 5 September 1885, while on leave of absence at Hamilton, Virginia, he became seriously ill, suffering from "congestion of the liver, dyspepsia, nervous prostration, and impaired heart activity." This was aggravated by mental anxiety incident to his duty as president of a general court-martial then in session and repeated attacks of yellow fever, contracted while on duty in the southeast Atlantic. At 4:30 P.M. on 22 September 1885, while in a state of "temporary insanity," he committed suicide by cutting his throat with a straight razor. He was survived by his wife and four children.[25]

The *Lilly Dale,* the vessel that carried James Dickson and Tom Hernandez from New York City to Hantsport, Nova Scotia, continued to ply its trade along the northeast coast. On 9 November 1863 it went aground on Old Proprietor Ledge, a rocky shoal at the entrance to the Bay of Fundy, broke up, and sank. The captain and crew were rescued and taken to Eastport, Maine.[26]

And what became of the *Standard* and its crewmen? Most of the men seem to have faded into the mists of time. Perhaps they served on other blockade runners as did Tom Hernandez. But what became of the *Standard*? Was the vessel ever salvaged or reutilized? We may never know for certain, but on 30 May 1862, one month after the vessel had been sunk and burned, Mary Jones wrote in a letter to Lieutenant Jones, "You know the Halifax brig (after which the enemy invaded our river) was sunk at Busby's Landing. Captain Thomson [of the Liberty Rangers] is removing her ropes, etc., etc. and I am told pronounces her a staunch, well-built vessel. Only her upper works were burnt, and she floats at every high tide. Why could we not use her for our coast defense —give her a coat of iron, a lining of cotton bales, a boarding prow, a strong engine, a few big guns; man her with brave hearts; and let her go forth from our quiet little stream (where it seems to me this might be done as well as elsewhere) to make her mark upon our insolent foes? No, my son, if you think anything can be done to use this vessel for the purpose, speak of the matter to the proper authorities."[27] Whether or not the *Standard* was ever utilized or salvaged has not been determined. Perhaps there yet remains another chapter of the *Standard*'s story to be told. However, Mary Jones's quote does give clear indication as to the condition of the vessel a month after it had been sunk, which is something of a tribute to the hardiness of the *Standard* and the quality of its construction. But do the remains of the *Standard* still rest on the bottom of the North Newport River? If so, then it probably remains in pieces. The sunken *Standard* would have completely obstructed the channel of the river at that point, effectively blocking any major navigation of the river, which was why it was sunk in the first place. Before the war the North Newport had been regularly navigated by small coastal steamers that served the local planters and the

communities of Riceboro and Dorchester. These steamers ceased operations during the war, but by Christmas of 1865 they were running
again three times a week to Sunbury. Two months later they were navigating the North Newport all the way to Riceboro.[28] In order to navigate
the stream past Melon Bluff, the wreck of the *Standard* would had to have
been broken up so as not to present a hazard in the channel. Perhaps
this work was being done while the steamers were sailing to Sunbury
that winter of 1865.

There are also indications that some of the *Standard's* timbers may
have been salvaged and used to build a house on Colonel's Island many
years after the war. However, some modern-day residents of Liberty
County are known to regard the wreck of the old "blockade runner"
at Melon Bluff as one of their best fishing spots. Do the bones of the
Standard remain in the murky depths of the North Newport River?
Again, this may never be known for certain.

After Tom Hernandez left the *Standard,* he signed on the schooner
Agnes, which was at Darien. They ran the blockade through Doboy
Sound, avoiding the *Wamsutta,* in late May 1862, sailed to Nassau, then
ran the blockade of Savannah on their return trip. On 5 July 1862
Hernandez piloted the *Agnes* and a cargo of cotton out of Savannah and
through the blockade, but the sailors were captured three days later
off Hole-in-the-Wall near Nassau by the USS *Huntsville.*[29]

The *Agnes* was taken to Key West, Florida, and sold. The disposition
of the crew and passengers is not known, but Tom Hernandez must
have been a resourceful man. When he was freed, he made for Nassau, where, strangely enough, he found the *Agnes* waiting for a pilot to
run the blockade. Hernandez took the vessel out again, but his run
of luck seemed to have deserted him. On the afternoon of 25 September 1862, the *Agnes* was again captured, this time by the USS *Florida,* as
it tried to slip into St. Andrew's Sound. Ironically, on 29 September
1862 Hernandez and five others taken aboard the *Agnes* were transferred aboard the *Wamsutta* in Doboy Sound and confined there for
several days. Perhaps James Dickson was with these men. On 2 October 1862 they were taken to St. Simons Sound and sent aboard the
USS *Massachusetts* for transportation north.[30]

But Tom Hernandez was a determined individual. By December
1862 he was back in Savannah, having been released or exchanged, and

The Confederate ironclad CSS Atlanta, built at Savannah from the blockade runner Fingal. Hernandez served as one of two pilots aboard the ironclad and was injured when the pilot house was struck by a shell from the U.S. monitor Weehawken during operations in Wassaw Sound, Georgia, on 17 June 1863 that resulted in the capture of the vessel. Courtesy of the National Archives.

found his way through the blockade again. Although Hernandez had been continually active in piloting blockade runners, he was still on detached duty from the Confederate army to serve in that capacity. However, that December 1862 he was officially transferred from the 13th Georgia Battalion to the C.S. Navy to serve as a pilot. During this time the Southerners at the Savannah Navy Yard were completing the construction of a massive ironclad warship that had been converted from the blockade runner *Fingal.* When the ironclad was finished, it was named the CSS *Atlanta,* and Tom Hernandez was assigned as one of the ship's two pilots.[31]

On the night of 16 June 1863, the *Atlanta* left its anchorage at Thunderbolt and proceeded downriver toward Wassaw Sound to engage the Federal blockaders. Two U.S. monitor ironclads, the USS *Weehawken* and the USS *Nahant,* were lying in wait. On the afternoon of 17 June 1863 the *Atlanta* steamed into Wassaw Sound and maneuvered into a firing position while closing with the Federal ironclads. Suddenly the

U.S. Navy officers aboard the Confederate ironclad Atlanta *after its capture and inclusion in the U.S. Navy. The pilot house where Tom Hernandez was wounded when the vessel was captured is clearly visible between the two men standing atop the casement at center rear. Courtesy of the National Archives.*

Hernandez, the bearded gentleman reclining in the first row, is photographed with members of the crew of the CSS Atlanta *during their stay at Fort Warren in Boston harbor. Courtesy of the National Archives.*

Atlanta ran hard aground on a mudbank near Cabbage Island, and nothing could extract the monster from the mud. The *Weehawken* sent several shells at the *Atlanta,* which could not return fire because the list of the vessel prevented its guns from being brought to bear. One of the *Weehawken's* shells struck the *Atlanta's* pilot house atop the vessel, taking off the roof and wounding the two helmsmen and two pilots inside.[32]

Just how badly Hernandez was wounded has not been determined. He was captured with the *Atlanta* and its crew and detained at Hilton Head, where he was hospitalized with other wounded Confederate sailors. When Hernandez began to recover, he was sent to rejoin the crew of the *Atlanta,* then being held at Fort LaFayette in New York City, where he was further hospitalized. On 23 July 1863 they were all transferred to Fort Warren on George's Island in the Boston harbor for further incarceration. While at Fort Warren, many of the prisoners from the *Atlanta* sat for individual portraits taken by a Boston photographer, and in the fall of 1864, just prior to an exchange of prisoners, many of the crewmen and officers of the *Atlanta* sat for group photographs. These provide one of the few known glimpses of Tom Hernandez.

Hernandez was exchanged on 1 October 1864 and was back in Savannah by month's end. At this time he was now being carried on the rolls of the Confederate navy, and on 27 October he was ordered to the ironclad CSS *Savannah* to serve as pilot. On 4 December he was ordered to the gunboat CSS *Isondiga* and was serving at the Savannah Navy Yard when Sherman's army closed on Savannah. When that city was evacuated, Hernandez was sent to the Charleston Navy Yard for a short time in early January 1865 before being ordered to the Augusta Navy Yard on 5 January 1865.[33]

After the war Hernandez returned to Savannah, where he continued to work as a river pilot for many years. He died on 7 March 1903 at the age of eighty-one and was buried in Laurel Grove Cemetery. Today the plot where his grave is located is marked, but Hernandez's grave itself is unmarked.[34]

And what became of James Dickson, whose diary provided the key to unlock the puzzle of the *Standard* and its journey? He apparently did not enlist in any military units or take any active role in the war

The Hernandez plot in Laurel Grove Cemetery, Savannah, Georgia, where records indicate Tom Hernandez was buried. Photograph by the author.

that was raging at that time, as there are no military records to document his enlistment. He may have remained in Savannah after the *Standard's* destruction, but in all probability he accompanied Tom Hernandez on the *Agnes*. Just how many other blockade runners Dickson might have served on is unknown, but at some point he did successfully run out through the blockade, for in August 1864 he was back at Birch Cove, Nova Scotia, where he married Peter and Susannah Donaldson's daughter Emma on 10 August 1864.[35] Although they were apparently very happy together, their lives would be plagued by tragedy.

It appears that they remained at Birch Cove, for the following year James and Emma Dickson's first child, James Bernard, was born there, but lived only a short time, passing away that same year.[36] The following year they had a daughter, Mary Grace, whom they called "Minnie."[37] By this time the Dicksons had returned to Newark, New Jersey, where they took up residence with his parents at 1 Washington Place.[38] The couple visited Birch Cove frequently, and on occasion he traveled to Savannah on business for his father.[39] In 1868 Dickson's father passed away, and his remains were sent to Savannah to rest in Laurel Grove Cemetery with Dickson's little sister. In 1869 Dickson moved

The Dickson family plot in Laurel Grove Cemetery, Savannah, Georgia, a scant few yards down the same lane where Tom Hernandez is buried. Photograph by the author.

his family down the street to 8 Washington Place.[40] That same year their next child, James Gordon Dickson, joined them, having been born at Birch Cove when Emma returned there to be with her family during the final weeks of her pregnancy.[41] In 1871 Dickson purchased eighty-three acres of land from the Donaldsons at Birch Cove and built a house there where the family could spend their summer visits. This also might have been brought on by the birth of their third child, Norman Donaldson Dickson, who was born at Birch Cove in 1871. Their last child, Emma Gertrude Dickson, known as "Gertie," was also born at Birch Cove, in 1875.[42]

Dickson lived to see his children born and enjoyed their early years; however, after Gertie's birth he began to suffer from ill health. He died at the age of forty-two in Newark on 30 September 1878. His body was returned to Savannah to repose in the Dickson family plot at Laurel

Grove Cemetery, fifty feet down the same lane from where Tom Hernandez was to be buried twenty-five years later. His son James Gordon apparently had his father's love for the sea and became a sailor, working on merchant vessels. However, his career was a short one, for in 1888, at the age of nineteen, he fell overboard and was lost at sea. This tragedy was followed up the next year in 1889 when the youngest child, Emma Gertrude, dear "Gertie," passed away in Newark at the age of fourteen, probably from one of the infectious diseases that made the rounds every so often. She was buried at Birch Cove. Only Norman and Minnie remained with their mother. Emma and children remained in Newark for a number of years after Dickson's death; however, living in the Washington Place house was a constant reminder of their family tragedies. Minnie wrote to her cousin Nellie at Birch Cove in September 1890, "The very best rooms in the house remind us of death. Poor Pa died in one front bedroom, Gertie in the other, Jim and Norman had the front room higher up and Pa, Grandpa, Gertie, were taken out of the parlors and while they were sick, sad things happened in other of the rooms and to be here keeps us in mind of our dreadful trouble all the time."[43] Eventually Emma relocated to 137 4th Avenue in Newark. However, by the turn of the century, she and Minnie and Norman returned to Nova Scotia, where they would live out their lives.[44]

Dickson noted in his diary on 6 January 1862, while he and Hernandez were at Birch Cove prior to their departure aboard the *Standard*, "I think that our privations and disappointments in life only be-fit us to appreciate with real pleasure the little enjoyments that are here and there scattered along our road to eternity, and I am sure Heaven will be none the less bright and happy, from its contrast with this dark world of trouble and contention that we will leave behind us."

SEVEN

Postlude

As the succeeding years passed on so did those individuals who were involved in the events that transpired on the North Newport River in 1862, but they left behind letters and other mementos of their presence during those chaotic times. The Jones family letters eventually ended up in several archive and library holdings in Georgia and Louisiana. James Dickson's diary apparently made its way to Nova Scotia when Emma and the children returned there after his death in Newark, New Jersey, in 1878.[1] Emma passed away at Birch Cove on 24 July 1930, and Minnie joined her in 1954. The diary remained in the possession of Norman Donaldson Dickson, who resided at Birch Cove until his death there in April 1957. Since Norman and his wife had no children and his wife pre-deceased him in 1950, he willed his home to Harry Sieniewicz, who was an antiques dealer.[2]

However, James Dickson's diary was apparently obtained from Norman at Birch Cove in 1954 by Sieniewicz, who sold it to a friend, Lawrence B. Romaine, a dealer of Americana from Middleboro, Massachusetts. He published an article about it in the spring 1955 issue of *Manuscript* magazine. This article was brought to the attention of William P. Kellam, a friend of Romaine's and director of libraries at the University of Georgia. Kellam contacted Romaine regarding the availability of the diary. and in July 1956 the University of Georgia purchased the diary from Romaine for 250 dollars.

Kellam conducted extensive research into the background and family of James Dickson and the story his diary relates, but he was unable to establish any facts concerning the fate of the blockade runner on which Dickson sailed, other than to record what he regarded as a legend: that it had been burned to prevent its capture. He assumed that the reason the diary ends so abruptly had something to do with the vessel's destruction but could not document when that destruction occurred. After several years of research and correspondence with various people and archival agencies, Kellam discontinued his efforts, and the diary was returned to the university manuscript collection, where it remained for almost twenty years as an interesting but incomplete document.

In 1974 I began picking up the pieces of the puzzle from a different perspective than that pondered by Kellam. At the time I was employed by the Georgia Department of Natural Resources as superintendent of the Midway Museum State Historic Site in Liberty County, Georgia. The focus of the museum was primarily the Colonial and Revolutionary War periods, but my personal interests lay in Civil War history, and there was a lot of it in coastal Georgia, sometimes overshadowed by other events. The biggest Civil War event to hit Midway, Georgia, was the arrival of Sherman's soldiers in December 1864. However, I wondered if the first hostilities in Liberty County had not come before Sherman's men. For three years prior to that, the U.S. Navy had been active on the coast, landing raiding parties, confiscating slaves, and burning everything from salt works to entire communities. The threat of unannounced violence turning up on one's doorstep was very real to the Southerners who resided on the coast during that time. Their enemy was visible every day in the form of the U.S. Navy gunboats that blockaded their coast.

During the course of researching local Civil War history, I came across the first piece of information that sparked my initial interest. This was William A. Fleming's unpublished manuscript "Reminiscences of the Liberty Independent Troop," written in 1896 and kept in the library of the Midway Museum. In this he briefly describes the invasion of the North Newport River, the destruction of the blockade runner, and the exchange of gunfire between the Liberty Independent Troop and the two navy gunboats at Half Moon Bluff.

Fleming's account of the incident was limited, so I looked into the *Official Records of the Union and Confederate Navies in the War of the Rebellion,* where I located Lt. Cmdr. Semmes's report of the event. This gave me a good insight into the perspective from the decks of the gunboats. In Robert Manson Myers's *The Children of Pride* I located the Reverend Charles C. Jones's letter that described this incident from his perspective and gave me some insight into how the inhabitants of the area had seen the invasion of their river.

Gradually, the more I looked into this event, the more I began to see a multidimensional view emerge. However, one important piece of the picture was missing and seemed forever lost. There was little information about the blockade runner that had been the catalyst for the affair at Half Moon Bluff, other than a mention in one of the Jones's letters that it had come from Halifax, Nova Scotia. I gave up looking further when I considered the insignificance of the entire incident, yet the mystery of the thing continued to nag me, and I often paused at Half Moon Bluff to ponder the events of those April days in 1862, events that no one else was even aware of, much less the people who live there today. When I looked beyond the new homes and marinas that line the bluff today, I could not help but wonder if, somewhere, there might be a logbook or a document from that nameless blockade runner that would reveal the missing part of the picture.

There seemed to be little point in pursuing further research. I did not even know where to start looking for information about an anonymous ship that ran the blockade of the Georgia coast more than a century before. It appeared to be a matter of seeking the proverbial needle in a haystack without knowing if there was a needle to be found in there. Thus I all but forgot the incident at Half Moon Bluff and the unknown blockade runner.

Three years later, in February 1977, I was on a research visit to the University of Georgia Library in Athens, where I had been surveying the manuscript collection catalog to see what material the library had that would be of interest to some other research I was doing. As I made my way through the card catalog, I came across a card for the James Dickson diary. The catalog card said that the diary related the journey of a young Georgian on a blockade runner from Halifax, Nova Scotia, and that it was an incomplete document, ending in mid-sentence.

No one knew the outcome of the account that was recorded. I never dared hope that it could be the same blockade runner since so many were run out of Halifax. The odds seemed pretty long that this diary could in any way relate to my blockade runner, but I felt that it might give me some insight, so I checked it out.

When I received the small, leather-bound volume with the man's name embossed on the front, I realized that it would take a good deal of time to wade through it in order to glean whatever pearls of knowledge might be there. I was surprised to find the first entry opening in Newark, New Jersey, in December 1861. This seemed odd when I considered that this was supposed to have been kept by a young man from Georgia. I turned to the back of the diary to see when the last entry was made. A chill ran up my spine when I realized that the last entry was dated only three weeks before the blockade runner incident I had researched. But the box that held the diary also contained a number of papers from someone else's research and a typed transcript of the diary. I invested in having a copy of the transcript made so I could take it home and read it.

When I got home, I read the transcript and cross-referenced the information with my charts of the Georgia coast, my maps of the area, and my previous research on the incident. Within a few hours I knew it. By some strange twist of fate, I found that I had indeed accidently stumbled on my lost blockade runner. I knew who was there and had their whole story before me. Subsequent research confirmed undeniably that it was so. I had found the piece of the puzzle that Kellam had searched for and that the University of Georgia Library held. We had pondered the same puzzle from opposite ends, twenty years apart. Thus, when all the information was put together, James Dickson's story emerged from the oblivion where it had been hidden for more than a century. It was a queer feeling that swept over me that night in February 1977, when I realized that I was the only person alive who knew the story of this little piece of history. I knew it had to be told.

What prevented the two pieces of the puzzle from being reunited was the sudden and abrupt end of Dickson's narrative. Why does the diary narrative end suddenly in mid-sentence, in mid-page, like a novel with the last chapter torn out? A possible answer to this question is hypothetical but based on practical evidence. The sudden halt in the narrative is probably a result more of human nature than any human drama connected with the journey of the *Standard*. It appears that the Dickson diary in the University of Georgia Library is a recopied version done in later years by James Dickson from the diary he actually kept on the journey.

In his vivid descriptions of the storms they passed through on their voyage, Dickson frequently states that almost everything and everyone aboard was soaked with water, yet the diary in the University of Georgia Library shows absolutely no water damage. Indeed, it is written in such smooth, even handwriting that one wonders where, on a ship being tossed about like a cork on the raging Atlantic, would Dickson have found a dry place to write the diary entries in the steady, even handwriting that the diary exhibits. Perhaps the diary he actually kept was so weather-worn that at some later date he began to recopy it. The diary in the University of Georgia Library is in James Dickson's handwriting, as is evidenced by his signature on the inside front cover and the signature on his will, which are identical. The fact remains that the diary was written by James Dickson but could not be the one he carried on the *Standard*.

There is other evidence. The diary is inscribed inside the back cover in a faded pencil script that states, "August 23, 1862 To J.D. from Wm H.H.Y." This indicates that someone presented this particular diary book to James Dickson some four months after he left the *Standard*. A search of the Savannah City Directory for 1866 shows that there was a W. H. H. Yonge (William Henry Harrison Yonge) living there at that time who was a printer and bookbinder. He is probably the same man who gave the diary book to Dickson.

There are also seven pages that have been cut out of the book in the middle of Dickson's narrative about the *Standard*, yet these missing pages, which show evidence of writing on the stubs, do not affect the story that Dickson has recorded. This seems to indicate that something that had been written in the book was judged to be unimportant or incorrect and removed prior to the copying of the narrative concerning the *Standard*.

Certain portions of the Dickson narrative also indicate that it had been recopied with a foreknowledge of events to come. As an example, in the very early part of the narrative, as the *Standard* was preparing to go into the first storm, Dickson recorded, "Although now severe we have only commenced what we shall for some time be compelled to endure, dangers, trials and hardship upon a small and disabled craft some three to four hundred miles eastward and making lee-way rapidly." This seems to indicate that the diary had been rewritten at a later point in time, and there are several other such examples that appear throughout the narrative.

And so, as the evidence makes clear, the diary manuscript in the University of Georgia Library is a copy written in Dickson's own hand, made from his original diary, which has since become lost to us. Apparently Dickson arrived at a point in recopying where he ceased and never again picked up the pen. But the diary's copy provides us with enough of the *Standard*'s story, for now the other half of the story, which Dickson neglected to copy, is known to us. Perhaps today, somewhere in Nova Scotia, James Dickson's original diary lies undiscovered and unappreciated. Maybe Dickson's original diary did not survive into this century and was long ago relegated to the waste can or consumed by some other misfortune. It makes one wonder just what parts of the story have been lost to us today because Dickson did not finish copying the diary. Perhaps he and Tom Hernandez participated in many more blockade-running adventures after leaving the *Standard,* adventures that were detailed in the original diary, adventures that are unknown to us now.

But the story that unravels on the yellowed pages of the diary is one of tremendous excitement. The reader is quickly swept up in the events while reading of Dickson's thoughts and experiences aboard ship. He was very descriptive and paid close attention to details. The reader feels as though he or she is seeing it all through Dickson's eyes, hearing with his ears, feeling with his senses, and being privy to his private thoughts. The reader can almost smell the salt air, feeling the wind against his or her face and the rolling of the deck beneath his or her feet. Becoming acquainted with the other crewmen and passengers, the reader also becomes a vicarious passenger.

It was a curious feeling that swept over me on that night in February 1977, when I realized that the diary transcript I had been reading was actually related to the same blockade runner that had caused the difficulties in Liberty County in April 1862. I realized at that moment that I was probably the only person alive who knew this story of Dickson, Hernandez, the *Standard,* and the events that transpired. It was then that I was propelled on my own journey, motivated by James Dickson's diary.

I wanted to verify some geographic locations on the Georgia coast to determine if my calculations from Dickson's diary were correct, so I called on my good friend Lynn Holman of Colonel's Island to assist me with a series of expeditions. Lynn was a long-time resident of the area and at that time was employed on St. Catherine's Island. With his boat and knowledge of the inland waterways, we were well prepared. Our first expedition was to St. Catherine's, where Lynn took me to the site of the Waldburg South End House, where the ruins of tabby slave cabins still remain. To my delight, there, stretching across the marsh, were the definite remnants of an oyster shell causeway leading to the river. It was the causeway that James Dickson and his friends were crossing when the diary narrative ceased. From the water side we approached the point where the causeway reached the river and were able to get out of the boat and walk on it for some distance. I felt the presence of James Dickson, for I stood in his footsteps.

Another expedition took us to the north end of Blackbeard Island, today a National Wildlife Refuge. We had to anchor Lynn's boat a short distance out because of the imminent fall of the tide, however our foray was a short one. Maps indicated an artesian well on the north end of the island; if this was also the location of Civil War earthworks, this would correspond exactly to what Dickson had noted. We hiked up into the trees and almost immediately came upon an earthen mound with an iron Civil War gun truck still sitting in place and the carriage pushed off to one side. This was totally unexpected, and I took photographs. A short time later we located the artesian well directly behind the gun position. Our mission accomplished, we hiked out, only to find, much to our dismay, that Lynn's boat was almost totally beached and the tide was dropping rapidly. We struggled and struggled, but the water was going away too fast to get enough of it under the boat to float it. There was no getting around it. We were stranded on the beach at Blackbeard Island, just like James Dickson had been a century earlier.

We did not care to wait for the tide to turn, and by rummaging around the debris line along the beach, we found a number of round wooden fence poles. Using these as rollers, we were able to get the boat back in the water and on our way. The gun carriage and truck we located turned out to be of the proper vintage but had been placed in the Civil War battery during the Spanish-American War. The National Park Service eventually recovered this equipment, and today it can be seen at Fort Pulaski National Monument at the mouth of the Savannah River.

On another expedition we made the run up the North Newport River to see the sights as the *Standard* and the gunboats would have seen them. We landed at Melon Bluff, which we found thick with undergrowth. Again I felt the presence of James Dickson, for he had been there. We went on up the North Newport to the boat landing at Montevideo Plantation, where Joseph Jones had hailed the passing boat from the *Standard* as it went up to Riceboro after they had left the ship for good.

We made trips to Savannah to track down the location of the LaRoche and Bell warehouse on Bay Street and the homes where Tom Hernandez lived over the years. And, in the end, we went to Laurel Grove Cemetery to pay our respects to Dickson and Hernandez. Finally, after all of these forays into historical detective work, I knew I had everything I needed to make an indisputable case. But I also began to realize that I had only covered half the distance. At some point in time, I would have to go to the northeast and track Dickson's travels from Newark, New Jersey, to the shores of Nova Scotia. I conducted some research through the mail, writing to various agencies and archives in Nova Scotia where I got information and made some contacts, but there were many questions I could not answer without going there myself. It was as though Dickson was calling to me, and I felt compelled to go. Thus, I began a journey with James Dickson as my spiritual companion.

My wife and I departed Augusta, Georgia, on the evening of 15 September 1978, heading for New York City, where we stayed with friends residing there. On 18 September 1978, we headed north, bound for the coast of Maine to go to the Cranberry Islands and find where the *Lilly Dale* had gone aground. The next morning we made our way into Northeast Harbor, where we caught the mail boat to Little Cranberry Island. Near the ferry landing on Little Cranberry was the

Isleford Historical Museum, where we were able to determine where the *Lilly Dale* went aground and the location of the rocks where the men of the *Lilly Dale* had seen another schooner foundering in the storm. The rocks were clearly visible, having had other rocks piled on them so as to expose the hazard and mark their location. My wife and I trudged down the long, gravel beach where the *Lilly Dale* had gone aground and thought about Dickson and Hernandez. In my mind's eye I could visualize this place as a frozen, snow-covered waste. After photographs were taken, we hiked back up the beach, feeling the presence of James Dickson very strongly.

We pressed northward that afternoon of 20 September, on to New Brunswick, Canada. We made stops at Musquash, where the *Lilly Dale* weathered a storm, and later we found a good vantage point to view Cape Split, which Dickson spoke of passing. By 4:00 P.M. we were pulling into Halifax, Nova Scotia. Over the next few days we visited Hantsport, Windsor, Halifax, and Birch Cove, which we found to be filled with streets and houses, much like any other suburb of any other large city. It was a beautiful setting with the heights sloping away from Bedford Basin and the tree cover broken here and there by roof lines and television antennas. While we had established that the Dicksons and the Donaldsons had owned most of Birch Cove at one time, their address remained the same over the years. It was always "Birch Cove." After speaking with several local residents, we were able to identify the Donaldson house. Although the current house stands on the site of the one Dickson and Hernandez visited, the Donaldsons had built a newer home on the site about 1901–3 for Mary "Minnie" Dickson.[3] I felt a warmth inside as I walked away, thinking about all the pleasant times that must have occurred there that were memories for Dickson but at which I could only wonder. I felt his presence ever so strongly as I stood in the yard of that house and looked at it.

We traveled on, retracing our route back to the States, and stopped for the night near Boston. We caught the boat to Fort Warren on George's Island on 23 September, where we located the spot where the photograph of the CSS *Atlanta's* crew had been taken in the fall of 1864. Tom Hernandez had been there. That afternoon we pressed on for New York City, stopping for a few days to investigate the location of the Dickson homes in Newark and the Brooklyn Navy Yard. Soon we were on our way south, and on 30 September 1978 we arrived back in Augusta after a long and fruitful journey to Nova Scotia. It was not until we pulled into Augusta that I realized the date was the one hundredth anniversary of James Dickson's death. Was it a coincidence?

I thought about how ironic it was that through Dickson's diary I had been able to experience an event in his life, rather like an invisible entity looking over his shoulder as he and Hernandez and their companions made their way through a series of adventures. Then, over a hundred years later, as I tracked his journey through his diary and traveled to the places he described, he became an invisible entity looking over my shoulder. Here was a young man of comparable age to my own who had lived his life a century before me, but his life and the events he lived still touched me.

I found myself to be the custodian of Dickson's story, and I set about trying to piece it all together and to preserve it in such a way that others could experience and enjoy it. Because of Dickson's efforts to record his experiences, we today can look at a slice of history as not only mere events and dates, but as the individual human realities that made up those events. Because of James Dickson's diary and a certain twist of fate, we can brush aside the years and once again stand on the deck of the *Standard* as it sweeps over the waves under full sail, bound for the Georgia coast, the Federal blockade, and its final destiny. And their trail, though a century old, can still be traced. Somehow I had found that needle in the haystack. Was it a coincidence? My trip to Nova Scotia taught me that there was no such thing as coincidence. It was a twist of fate.

NOTES

Abbreviations

CCC-60   The 1860 Census of Chatham Couny, Georgia

GDAH   Georgia Department of Archives and History, Atlanta

MM   Midway Museum, Midway, Georgia

MPR   Military Pension Records

MSR   Military Service Records

NA   National Archives

ORN   *Official Records of the Union and Confederate Navies*

RHS   Rockingham Historical Society, Halifax, Nova Scotia

TU   Tulane University, New Orleans, Louisiana

UGA   University of Georgia, Athens

Chapter 1—Prelude

1. Stern, *Confederate Navy*, 62. Carse, *Hilton Head Island in the Civil War*, 1.
2. *ORN*, series 1, 1:352.
3. Carse, *Hilton Head Island in the Civil War*, 12–18.
4. Ibid., 1–2.
5. Ibid., 3–4.
6. Ibid., 5–6.
7. Ibid., 12–18.
8. Cowley, *Leaves from a Lawyer's Life Afloat*, 13. Soley, *Blockade and the Cruisers*, 85.
9. Clark, *Under the Stars and Bars*, 80–81.
10. Groover, *Sweet Land of Liberty*, 44.
11. *ORN*, series 1, 2:288.
12. Carse, *Hilton Head Island in the Civil War*, 10–11.
13. CCC-60, 179.
14. Henderson, *Roster of the Confederate Soldiers of Georgia, 1861–1865*, 6:395.
15. *ORN*, series 1, 12:361. CCC-60, 61. Luke Christy was a native of New York. He died 1 January 1884 and was buried in Laurel Grove Cemetery, lot 1041.
16. *ORN*, series 1, 12:361.
17. Ibid.

Chapter 2—Bound for Nova Scotia

1. Savannah City Directory, 1860. Kellam, research notes in James Dickson diary file, Hargrett Rare Book and Manuscript Library, UGA.

2. Ibid.

3. Wolfe, *Nova Scotia Registry of Shipping with Standard Rules for Construction and Classification.* The *Lilly Dale* was registry no. 41552.

4. Sharon Ingalls, Rockingham Historical Society (RHS), Halifax, N.S., e-mail communication 13 January 2003.

5. The parenthesis here are James's. Was he perhaps refering to young Bridget Larman, the young Irish immigrant servant girl employed in the Dickson household?

6. James Dickson, diary, manuscript no. 791, in Hargrett Rare Book and Manuscript Library, UGA. Please note, since the focus of this book is Dickson's diary, it would be redundant to continue citing passages that are clearly from the diary. Thus the Dickson diary is cited only here, where it is first referenced.

7. The *Queen of Clippers* was built in 1859 and weighed 172 tons. It was registry no. 41552. The vessel was wrecked near Kingsboro, N.S., on the night of 31 December 1869.

8. *Gateway to the Valley*, 73.

9. Ibid.

10. Ibid., 82–83.

11. Ingalls, RHS, e-mail communication, 13 January 2003.

12. The girls James speaks of would have been the six Donaldson sisters, Jane, Katherine (Kate), Sarah Ann, Susan (Suzie), Helen, and Emma. Ingalls, RHS, e-mail communication, 13 January 2003.

Chapter 3—Bound for Georgia

1. Wolfe, registry no. 37859

2. Deals are lengths of lumber planking.

3. The fluid can was where the men urinated when they could not go up on deck to do so during a heavy storm.

4. The cargo of deals was buoyant and would float rather than sink. This vessel had taken on enough water to sink, but its cargo was bouyant enough to keep it afloat just below the surface of the water.

5. The "deep-sea-lead" was a device used for "sounding," or detecting the depth of water beneath the ship. The "lead-line" consisted of a long length of cord, knotted at certain intervals to mark units of measure, such as a knot to mark each foot of line. At the end of the cord was a heavy lead weight with an open cavity at the end. This cavity was filled with wax. The line would be thrown over the side and would go slack when the lead weight hit the bottom. By counting the number of knots in the line that were required to reach the bottom, or when the line was pulled in, an idea

of water depth could be established. The wax in the end of the lead weight would have a sample of the bottom composition embedded in it. This could be grains of sand, gravel, small bits of shell, or clay mud. Much could be learned by knowing what the bottom composition was, as well as the water depth.

6. This is quite likely a reference to Peter Williamson, *The Life, Travels, Voyages, and Daring Engagements of Paul Jones Containing Numerous Anecdotes of Undaunted Courage: To Which Is Prefixed, the Life and Adventures of Peter Williamson, Who Was Kidnapped When an Infant, from His Native Place, Aberdeen, and Sold for a Slave in America* (Albany, N.Y.: Printed by E. and E. Hosford, 1809).

7. CCC-60, 381.

Chapter 4—Results and Consequences

1. Bartholomew Austin Busby, born in the Orangeburg District of South Carolina on 10 August 1788, became a planter and by early manhood had accumulated slaves, much land, and associated wealth. He migrated to Liberty County, Georgia, where he settled at Melon Bluff on the North Newport River. The bluff took its name from the large amount of melons that had been shipped from there over a period of time. He became active in local affairs, joining the Liberty Independent Troop in 1822 and representing the county in the state legislature in 1834. On 14 November 1839, at the age of fifty-one, he married Mary Emeline Mallard. They had four daughters. Following the raid up the North Newport River in April of 1862, Busby removed his family and residence to Taylor's Creek in the upper part of the county. That December he died of typhoid pneumonia and was buried in the Midway Cemetery (Myers, *Children of Pride*, 1479–80).

2. Myers, ed., *A Georgian at Princeton*, 18.

3. Myers, *Children of Pride*, 1567.

4. Ibid., 1568.

5. Ibid.

6. Ibid., 20.

7. Joseph Jones, letters, TU. Letter to his wife Caroline, dated 23 October 1861.

8. Rev. Charles C. Jones, letter to Lt. Charles C. Jones Jr., 25 December 1861; Mrs. Mary Jones, letter to Lt. Charles C. Jones Jr., 16 April 1862; Rev. Charles C. Jones, letter to Lt. Charles C. Jones Jr., 21 April 1862. From Rev. Charles C. Jones Collection, Hargrett Rare Book and Manuscript Library, UGA. Joseph Jones, letter to his wife Caroline, dated 26 December 1861, TU.

9. Fleming, "Reminiscences of the Liberty Independent Troop," unpublished manuscript in the library of the Midway Museum, Midway, Ga.

10. *ORN*, series 1, 12:727.

11. Ibid.

12. Genealogies of Old Philadelphia Families, the Campbell Collection, vol. 4, p. 317–21, Historical Society of Pennsylvania, Philadelphia.

13. Ibid.

14. *ORN,* series 2, 1:183.

15. Logbook entry, USS *Potomska,* NA.

16. *ORN,* series 1, 12:728.

17. Logbook entry, USS *Potomska,* NA.

18. *ORN,* series 1, 12:756.

19. Mrs. Mary Jones, letter to Lt. Charles C. Jones Jr., 10 April 1862, UGA.

20. Logbook entry, USS *Potomska,* NA.

21. *ORN,* series 1, 12:757.

22. Mrs. Mary Jones, letter to Lt. Charles C. Jones Jr., 10 April 1862; Lt. Charles C. Jones Jr., letter to Mrs. Jones, 19 April 1862, UGA.

23. *ORN,* series 1, 12:744.

24. Logbook entry, USS *Potomska,* NA.

25. Mrs. Mary Jones, letter to Lt. Charles C. Jones Jr., 16 April 1862, UGA.

26. *ORN,* series 2, 1:235.

27. Ibid., series 1, 4:289.

28. Logbook entry, USS *Wamsutta,* NA.

29. Alexander Semmes, MSR, NA.

30. Logbook entry, USS *Wamsutta,* NA.

31. Logbook entry, USS *Potomska,* NA.

32. Ibid.

33. Ibid.

34. Ibid.

35. Fleming, "Reminiscences of the Liberty Independent Troop," MM.

36. Logbook entries, USS *Potomksa* and USS *Wamsutta,* NA.

37. Lt. Charles C. Jones Jr., letter to Mrs. Mary Jones, 19 April 1862, UGA.

38. Rev. Charles C. Jones, letter to Lt. Charles C. Jones Jr., 21 April 1862, UGA.

39. Logbook entry, USS *Wamsutta,* NA.

40. Logbook entry, USS *Potomska,* NA.

41. Ibid.

42. Fleming, "Reminiscences of the Liberty Independent Troop," MM.

43. Logbook entry, USS *Potomska,* NA.

Chapter 5—Time to Pay the Piper

1. Fleming, "Reminiscences of the Liberty Independent Troop," MM.

2. Logbook entry, USS *Potomska,* NA.

3. Rev. Charles C. Jones, letter to Lt. Charles C. Jones Jr., 28 April 1862, UGA.

4. The "Aunt Susan" mentioned here is the older sister of Rev. Charles C. Jones. She and her husband, William Henry Cumming, resided at a home on Colonel's Island, not far from Maybank, Reverend Jones's summer house. After the fall of Hilton Head on 7 November 1861, many coastal residents abandoned their island homes.

On 12 November, Reverend Jones and his sister's family closed their respective homes there and moved inland. Reverend Jones moved to his home at Montevideo, and his sister's family moved to Reverend Jones's plantation at Arcadia. Myers, *Children of Pride*, 793, 797, 800, 1499.

5. Joseph Jones, letter to his wife Caroline, 27 April 1862, TU.

6. James S. Warnell, diary, microform 2322, GDAH.

7. Logbook entry, USS *Potomska*, NA.

8. Joseph Jones, letter to his wife Caroline, 27 April 1862, TU.

9. Ibid.

10. Ibid., 7 November 1861.

11. Ibid., 27 April 1862.

12. Logbook entry, USS *Wamsutta*, NA.

13. Joseph Jones, letter to his wife Caroline, 27 April 1862, TU.

14. Logbook entry, USS *Potomska*, NA.

15. Ibid.

16. Logbook entry, USS *Wamsutta*, NA.

17. Logbook entry, USS *Potomska*, NA.

18. Joseph Jones, letter to his wife Caroline, 27 April 1862, TU.

19. Logbook entries, USS *Potomska* and USS *Wamsutta*, NA.

20. Ibid.

21. Joseph Jones, letter to his wife Caroline, 27 April 1862, TU.

22. Logbook entries, USS *Potomska* and USS *Wamsutta*, NA.

23. Joseph Jones, letter to his wife Caroline, 27 April 1862, TU.

24. Ibid.

25. *Halifax Evening Express*, 20 June 1862.

26. Logbook entries, USS *Potomska* and USS *Wamsutta*, NA.

27. Ibid.

28. Joseph Jones, letter to his wife Caroline, 27 April 1862, TU.

29. Rev. Charles C. Jones, letter to Lt. Charles C. Jones Jr., 28 April 1862, UGA.

30. Joseph Jones, letter to his wife Caroline, 27 April 1862, TU.

31. Rev. Charles C. Jones, letter to Lt. Charles C. Jones Jr., 28 April 1862, UGA.

32. Logbook entries, USS *Potomska* and USS *Wamsutta*, NA.

33. Warnell, diary, microform 2322, GDAH.

34. *ORN*, series 1, 12:776–77. Logbook entries, USS *Potomska* and USS *Wamsutta*, NA.

35. Logbook entries, USS *Wamsutta*, NA.

36. Joseph Jones, letter to his wife Caroline, 27 April 1862, TU.

37. Rev. Charles C. Jones, letter to Lt. Charles C. Jones Jr., 28 April 1862, UGA.

38. Warnell, diary, microform 2322, GDAH.

39. Logbook entries, USS *Potomska* and USS *Wamsutta*, NA.

40. Joseph Jones, letter to his wife Caroline, 27 April 1862, TU.

41. This was the Reverend David Lyman Buttolph and his wife Laura Elizabeth Maxwell, who was the daughter of Susan Mary (Jones) Cumming and her first husband, Audley Maxwell. Thus, she was Reverend Jones's neice. Reverend Buttolph was the minister of the Midway Church. Myers, *Children of Pride*, 1481.

42. Rev. Charles C. Jones, letter to Lt. Charles C. Jones Jr., 28 April 1862, UGA.

43. Ibid.

44. *ORN*, series I, 12:776–77.

45. Warnell, diary, microform 2322, GDAH.

46. Rev. Charles C. Jones, letter to Lt. Charles C. Jones Jr., 28 April 1862, UGA.

47. Fleming, "Reminiscences of the Liberty Independent Troop," MM.

48. Rev. Charles C. Jones, letter to Lt. Charles C. Jones Jr., 28 April 1862, UGA.

49. Logbook entries, USS *Potomska* and USS *Wamsutta*, NA.

50. Fleming, "Reminiscences of the Liberty Independent Troop," MM.

51. James Brown, George Boswell, MSR, NA.

52. *ORN*, series I, 12:776.

53. Fleming, "Reminiscences of the Liberty Independent Troop," MM.

54. *ORN*, series I, 12:776–77.

55. Joseph Jones, letter to his wife Caroline, 27 April 1862, TU.

56. Fleming, "Reminiscences of the Liberty Independent Troop," MM.

57. *ORN*, series I, 12:776–77.

58. Logbook entries, USS *Potomska* and USS *Wamsutta*, NA. James Brown, George Boswell, Surgeon's Report, MSR, NA.

59. James Brown, George Boswell, Surgeon's Report, MSR, NA.

60. Joseph Jones, letter to his wife Caroline, 27 April 1862, TU.

61. Rev. Charles C. Jones, letter to Lt. Charles C. Jones Jr., 28 April 1862, UGA.

62. Warnell, diary, microform 2322, GDAH.

63. Logbook entry, USS *Wamsutta*, NA. George Boswell, MSR, NA

64. Rev. Charles C. Jones, letter to Lt. Charles C. Jones Jr., 28 April 1862, UGA.

65. Logbook entry, USS *Wamsutta*, NA. James Brown, MSR, NA.

Chapter 6—Aftermath

1. Logbook entries, USS *Potomska* and USS *Wamsutta*, NA.

2. Joseph Jones, letter to his wife Caroline, dated 27 April 1862, TU.

3. Rev. Charles C. Jones, letter to Lt. Charles C. Jones Jr., 28 April 1862, UGA

4. Logbook entry, USS *Wamsutta*, NA.

5. *ORN*, series I, 12:775–76.

6. Rev. Charles C. Jones, letter to Lt. Charles C. Jones Jr., 28 April 1862, UGA.

7. *Halifax Evening Express,* 20 June 1862.

8. Lt. Charles C. Jones Jr., letter to Rev. Charles C. Jones, 30 April 1862, UGA.

9. Rev. Charles C. Jones, letter to Mrs. Eliza Robarts, 13 December 1862, UGA.

10. Myers, *Children of Pride,* 1480.

11. Rev. and Mrs. Charles C. Jones, letter to Lt. Charles C. Jones Jr., 22 May 1862, UGA.

12. Myers, *Children of Pride,* 1567–68.

13. Ibid., 1574–75.

14. Ibid.

15. Ibid.

16. Ibid., 1568.

17. Ibid.

18. Ibid., 1573.

19. *ORN,* series 2, 1:183.

20. Pendleton G. Watmough, MSR, MPR, NA.

21. Ibid.

22. *ORN,* series 2, 1:235.

23. Alexander Semmes, MSR, MPR, NA.

24. Ibid.

25. Ibid.

26. Charles A. Armour, chief archivist, Killiam Memorial Library and Archives, Dalhousie University, Halifax, N.S.

27. Mrs. Mary Jones, letter to Lt. Charles C. Jones Jr., 30 May 1862, UGA.

28. Mrs. Mary Jones, letters to Mrs. Mary Mallard, 9 December 1865, 26 February 1866, UGA.

29. *ORN,* series 1, 13:346–347.

30. Ibid.

31. Ibid.

32. Ibid. Lawrence, *Present for Mr. Lincoln,* 127.

33. Henderson, 6:395. Also ORN 1, 16:493–96.

34. Cemetery register for Laurel Grove Cemetery, Savannah, Ga., and Savannah newspaper obituaries, GHS. Tom is buried in lot 184.

35. Emma Donaldson was James Dickson's cousin. Ingalls, RHS, e-mail communication, 6 June 2003. Also noted in Kellam's research material.

36. Ingalls, RHS, e-mail communication, 4–6 June 2003.

37. Emma Donaldson Dickson, letter to her sister Helen, 13 January 1868. RHS.

38. Emma Donaldson Dickson, letter to her mother, Susannah, 10 January 1865. RHS.

39. Ibid.

40. Newark City Directory, 1869.

41. Ingalls, RHS, e-mail communication, 7 June 2003.
42. Ibid.
43. Ingalls, RHS, e-mail communication, 9 June 2003.
44. Noted in Kellam's research material.

Chapter 7—Postlude

1. Sharon Ingalls, e-mail communication, 7 June 2003.
2. Ibid., 9 June 2003.
3. Ibid., 7 June 2003.

BIBLIOGRAPHY

Books

Breeden, James O. *Joseph Jones, M.D., Scientist of the Old South.* Lexington: University Press of Kentucky, 1975.

Carse, Robert. *Hilton Head Island in the Civil War, Department of the South.* Columbia, S.C.: State Printing Company, 1961.

Clark, Walter A. *Under the Stars and Bars.* Augusta, Ga.: Chronicle Printing Company, 1900.

Cowley, Charles. *Leaves from a Lawyers Life Afloat.* Boston: Penhallow Printing, 1879.

Gateway to the Valley. Windsor, N.S.: Published by the Centennial Committee, 1977.

Genealogical Committee of the Georgia Historical Society. *The 1860 Census of Chatham County, Georgia.* Easley, S.C.: Southern Historical Press, 1980.

Geneaologies of Old Philadelphia Families, Vol. 3. N.p.: North American Publishing, 1909.

Hayes, John D., ed. *Samuel Francis Du Pont: A Selection from His Civil War Letters.* 3 vols. Ithaca, N.Y.: Published for the Eleutherian Mills Historical Library by Cornell University Press, 1969.

Henderson, Lillian. *Roster of the Confederate Soldiers of Georgia, 1861–1865.* 6 vols. Hapeville, Ga.: Longino and Porter, 1959–64.

Hill, Jim Dan. *The Civil War Sketchbook of Charles Ellery Stedman.* San Rafael, Calif.: Presidio Press, 1976.

Holland, Francis R., Jr. *America's Lighthouses.* Brattleboro, Vt.: Stephen Greene Press, 1972.

Jones, Charles C., Jr. *Historical Sketch of the Chatham Artillery during the Confederate Struggle for Independence.* Albany, N.Y.: Joel Munsell, 1867.

Lawrence, Alexander A. *A Present for Mr. Lincoln.* Macon, Ga.: Ardivan Press, 1961.

Mallard, Robert Q. *Montevideo—Maybank.* Richmond, Va., 1898.

Miller, Francis T. *The Photographic History of the Civil War.* 10 vols. New York: Thomas Yoseloff, 1901.

Murray, Alton J. *South Georgia Rebels.* Jacksonville, Fla.: Allied Printing, 1976.

Myers, Robert Manson. *The Children of Pride.* New Haven: Yale University Press, 1975.

———, ed. *A Georgian at Princeton.* New York: Harcourt Brace Jovanovich, 1976.

Official Records of the Union and Confederate Armies in the War of the Rebellion. 128 vols. Washington, D.C.: U.S. Government Printing Office, 1882–1900.

Official Records of the Union and Confederate Navies in the War of the Rebellion. Series 1, 27 vols.; series 2, 3 vols. Washington, D.C.: U.S. Government Printing Office, 1894–1922.

Register of Officers of the Confederate Navy. Washington, D.C.: U.S. Government Printing Office, 1898.

Smith, Derek. *Civil War Savannah.* Savannah, Ga.: Frederic C. Beil, 1997.

Soley, James R. *The Blockade and the Cruisers.* New York: C. Scribner's Sons, 1885.

Stern, Phillip Van Doren. *The Confederate Navy: A Pictorial History.* Garden City, N.Y.: Doubleday, 1962.

This They Remembered. Washington, Ga.: Washington Publishing Company, 1965.

Williamson, Peter. *The Life, Travels, Voyages, and Daring Engagements of Paul Jones Containing Numerous Anecdotes of Undaunted Courage: To Which Is Prefixed, the Life and Adventures of Peter Williamson, Who Was Kidnapped When an Infant, from His Native Place, Aberdeen, and Sold for a Slave in America.* Albany, N.Y.: Printed by E. and E. Hosford, 1809.

Wolfe, Thomas R. *Nova Scotia Registry of Shipping with Standard Rules for Construction and Classification.* Halifax, N.S.: A. Grant, 1866.

Ship Logbooks

U.S. Navy ship logbooks in the National Archives, Washington, D.C., for USS *Alabama*, USS *Potomska*, USS *Wamsutta*.

City Directories and Census Records

Chatham County, Georgia, Census Records, 1860 and 1866. Georgia Historical Society, Savannah, Ga.

Newark City Directories, 1860 and 1869. New Jersey Historical Society, Newark, N.J.

Philadelphia City Directory, 1860. Philadelphia City Library, Philadelphia, Pa.

Savannah City Directories, 1860 and 1866. Georgia Historical Society, Savannah, Ga.

Manuscripts and Letters

Ash, John. Diary. Robert W. Woodruff Library, Special Collections and Archives Division, Emory University, Atlanta, Ga.

Dickson, James. Diary. Hargrett Rare Book and Manuscript Library, University of Georgia, Athens.

Dickson Family Letters. Collection of correspondence between the Dicksons and Donaldsons, dating between 10 January 1865 and 20 February 1900. The Rockingham Historical Society, Halifax, N.S.

Fleming, William A. "Reminiscences of the Liberty Independent Troop." Unpublished manuscript. The library of the Midway Museum, Midway, Ga.

Jones, Rev. Charles C. Letters. Charles C. Jones Collection, Hargrett Rare Book and Manuscript Library, University of Georgia, Athens.

Jones, John. Letters. John Jones Collection, Hargrett Rare Book and Manuscript Library, University of Georgia, Athens.

Jones, Joseph. Letters. Joseph Jones Collection, Tulane University Library, New Orleans, La.

Warnell, James S. Diary, 1862–63. [microform 2322], Georgia Department of Archives and History, Atlanta, Ga.

Newspapers

Halifax (Nova Scotia) Evening Express, 20 June 1862.
Savannah Republican, 14, 15 April 1862.

Military Service and Pension Records, the National Archives, Washington, D.C.

Boswell, George, U.S.N.
Brown, James, U.S.N.
Lanier, Edmund, U.S.N.
Semmes, Alexander, U.S.N.
Watmough, Pendleton G., U.S.N.

INDEX

Agnes (steamer), 142, 151, 155
Alabama, USS, 97, 107, 108
Albion (schooner), 10, 11
Arcadia House, 31
Arcadia Plantation, 88, 93, 103, 111, 115, 125–27, 129, 131, 133, 140, 141, 146, 173
Atlanta, CSS, 152–54, 166
Augusta Navy Yard, 154
Avon River Bridge, 31, 32

Baker Island Light, 20, 21
Barnard, J. B., 89, 126, 128, 130, 132, 133
Ben (cook), 43, 44, 46, 56, 61, 64, 78, 80, 81, 83, 85
Birch Cove, N.S., 13, 32, 33, 35–38, 45, 155–58, 166
Blackbeard Island, Ga., 66, 70, 73, 76, 79, 100, 102, 164
Blanch, Captain, 39, 43, 46, 48, 50, 54, 56, 63, 65, 71, 74, 78, 87, 89, 93, 105, 117, 124–26, 130, 132
Boswell, George, 135, 137–39, 141, 142
Brooklyn Navy Yard, 98, 99, 166
Brown, James, 135, 137–39, 141
Brunswick, Ga., 8, 66
Busby, Bartholomew A., 89, 145, 171
Busby's Landing. *See* Melon Bluff, Ga.

Buttolph, David Lyman, 131, 134, 139, 174
Buttolph, Laura, 131

Calder, James R., 126, 146
Calder, Mrs., 130
Cape Blomidon, N.S., 28, 29
Cape Split, N.S., 25, 28, 29, 166
Carr's Neck, Ga., 88, 117, 118, 120–24, 134, 145
Cazier, Isabella, 9
Cazier, Maryann C. [Lamstad], 9
Charleston, S.C., 3, 4, 6, 9, 10, 12, 149
Charleston Navy Yard, 154
Charley (second mate), 44, 46, 59
Chatham Artillery, 91, 95, 142
Christy, Luke, 11, 169
Churchill, E. C. (shipyard), 13, 30
Clark, Walter A., 5
Collins, John, 31
Colonel's Island, Ga., 87, 88, 90, 91, 111–18, 123, 124, 128, 134, 137, 147, 151, 164, 171
Cranberry Islands, Me., 20, 21, 24, 25, 76, 165
Crowell, William, 19, 39
Cumberland Island, Ga., 66, 68
Cumberland Sound, Ga., 5

Daniel, A. B., 130
Darien, Ga., 66, 69, 80, 81, 85, 86, 99, 102, 132, 151

Darlington, USS, 144, 145
Day, John, 46, 48, 50, 56, 64, 73, 75–78, 81
Delta, RMS, 142
Dennis, John S., 99, 102
Dickson, Emma Donaldson, 156, 158
Dickson, Emma Gertrude, 156, 157
Dickson, James, 12–15, 23, 24, 30–41, 55, 57, 73, 74, 76, 77, 79, 80, 82, 83, 85, 93, 99–102, 105, 112, 142, 150, 151, 154–67
Dickson, James, Sr., 12
Dickson, James Bernard, 155, 157
Dickson, James Gordon, 156, 157
Dickson, Mary Grace, 156, 157, 166
Dickson, Norman Donaldson, 156–58
Doboy Island, Ga., 141, 142
Doboy Sound, Ga., 69, 102, 103, 105, 108, 110, 120, 122, 140–42, 149, 151
Donaldson, Emma, 34, 155, 156, 170
Donaldson, Helen, 34, 170
Donaldson, Jane, 33, 170
Donaldson, Katherine, 34, 170
Donaldson, Peter, 13, 33, 155
Donaldson, Sarah Ann, 34
Donaldson, Susan, 34, 170
Donaldson, Susannah, 13, 33, 155
Donaldson, Thomas, 34, 38, 39
Donaldson, William, 13, 38, 39
Dorchester, Ga., 88, 89, 101, 121, 128, 151
Dugan, 54, 55, 72, 75, 77, 78, 81–83, 86
Duke, W. H., 133
Du Pont, Samuel F., 3, 86, 97, 98, 105, 142

Fingal (steamer), 8, 9, 152
Fleming, Thomas L., 134

Fleming, William A., 109, 112, 114, 134, 135, 137, 159, 160
Florida, USS, 105, 107, 109, 151
Fort Beauregard, S.C., 4
Fort Clinch, Fla., 5
Fort Lafayette, N.Y., 154
Fort Pulaski, Ga., 4, 5, 97, 100–104, 165
Fort Walker, S.C., 4
Fort Warren, Mass., 10, 153, 154, 166
Four Mile House, N.S., 32, 33, 35
Fraser (sailor), 81, 83, 85
Frenchman's Bay, Me., 20–22, 24

Goldsborough, John R., 4, 105, 107, 109, 110
Gordon, George A., 9
Grace. *See* Grice
Grice (sailor), 133

Half Moon Bluff, Ga., 87, 89, 102, 113, 114, 116, 117, 122, 123, 134–38, 143, 145, 159, 160
Halifax, N.S., 13, 25, 30–38, 40–42, 142, 160, 161, 166
Handley, George, 120
Hantsport, N.S., 13, 18, 25, 29–31, 150
Hernandez, Thomas L., 9–16, 23, 24, 30–40, 54, 55, 69, 72, 75, 77, 78, 80, 81, 85, 86, 93, 99, 101, 102, 105, 142, 150–57, 163–67
Hilton Head Island, S.C., 3, 4, 6–9, 98, 118, 154
Hinesville, Ga., 66, 88, 116
Holman, Lynn, 164
Hughes, William, 132
Huntley, Daniel, 39, 118
Huntsville, USS, 151
Hutchinson (first mate), 52, 59, 61, 65, 78, 80

Iroquois, USS, 2
Isondiga, CSS, 154

Jones, Charles C., Jr., 90, 93–96,
    101, 105, 106, 110, 115, 125, 127,
    138, 141, 142, 144, 147, 150
Jones, Rev. Charles C., 89, 90,
    92–94, 96, 101, 103, 105, 107,
    110, 115, 122, 125, 127, 129, 131,
    133, 134, 138, 139, 141, 142, 145,
    146, 160, 172, 173
Jones, Joseph, 91, 93, 94, 101, 103,
    105–8, 110, 111, 115–27, 129, 130,
    132–35, 138–40, 143, 147, 148, 165
Jones, Mary, 89, 90, 93, 96, 97, 101,
    103, 105–7, 110, 115, 122, 125–27,
    141, 146, 147, 150
Jones, Mary Sharpe (Mallard), 90, 94,
    95, 146, 147

Kansas, USS, 148
Kellam, William P., 158, 159, 161
King, Audley Maxwell, 114, 127, 133,
    138
King, George F., 112
King, Julian C., 112
King, Mrs., 115, 116, 138
King, Roswell, III, 112.
King's Landing, 133

La Chatelet Plantation, 140
Lamar (tugboat), 10
Lanier, Edmund, 97, 99, 106–8
Larman, Bridget, 12, 170
LaRoche and Bell, 96, 103–5, 165
Lee, Robert E., 7, 8
Lehigh, USS, 149
Liberty Guards, 116, 127, 129, 132, 138
Liberty Independent Troop, 87, 91,
    105, 107, 109–12, 115–18, 124,
    127, 128, 133–35, 141, 159, 171

Liberty Rangers, 109, 110, 150
Lilly Dale (brigantine), 13–15, 17,
    19–22, 24, 26–29, 39, 99, 150,
    165, 166

Major (sailor), 18
Mallard, Mary Sharpe Jones. *See* Jones,
    Mary Sharpe (Mallard)
Mallard, Robert Q., 90, 95, 134, 139,
    146, 147
Mallow Plantation, 144
Martin, John A., 128
Massachusetts, USS, 151
Maxwell's Point (plantation), 112, 113,
    138
Maybank Plantation, 90, 91, 115, 147,
    172
McIntosh Station, Ga., 66, 88, 90,
    93, 100, 103, 128
McIver, Augustus Monroe, 112, 114,
    120
Melon Bluff, Ga., 88, 89, 93, 97,
    100, 103, 105, 113, 117–19, 126,
    128, 130, 132, 143, 150, 151, 165,
    171
Memphis, USS, 148
Michigan, USS, 98
Mississippi, USS, 98
Montevideo Plantation, 88–93, 96,
    97, 101, 103, 105–7, 110, 111, 113,
    115, 117, 122, 125–27, 129–34, 138,
    140, 141, 145–47, 165, 173
Mount Desert Rock (Island), Me., 20,
    21, 24
Musquash, N.B., 25, 26, 166

Nahant, USS, 152
Newark, N.J., 12–14, 156–58, 165
New York City, 11, 12, 101, 106, 150,
    166
North Newport Parade Ground, 109

North Newport River, Ga., 87, 89–91, 93, 101, 112, 114, 116, 118, 119, 122, 123, 126, 130, 131, 137, 138, 140, 144–46, 150, 151, 158, 159, 161, 165, 171

Oliver (sailor), 56

Paradise (schooner), 48
Penguin, USS, 10, 11
Phoenix Riflemen, 9
Philadelphia Navy Yard, 98, 106, 107, 138, 148, 149
Port Royal Sound, S.C., 3, 4, 6–9, 102, 105, 107–9, 118, 119
Potomska, USS, 98–103, 106–16, 120–25, 128, 129, 132, 134–37, 140, 141, 144, 145, 148

Queen of Clippers, 27, 170

Rhode Island, USS, 107
Riceboro, Ga., 66, 87–91, 93, 101, 110, 114–17, 126, 130–32, 150, 165
Romaine, Lawrence B., 158

Sabine, USS, 2
St. Andrews Sound, Ga., 151
St. Catherine's Island, Ga., 66, 70, 83, 86, 87, 97–99, 102, 111
St. Catherine's Sound, Ga., 100, 102, 105, 148, 164
St. Lawrence, USS, 10
St. Simons Island, Ga., 66, 70, 80, 97, 99, 106, 107
St. Simons Sound, Ga., 102, 105–9, 151
Sapelo Island, Ga., 66, 69, 70, 100, 102, 106–10, 140
Sapelo River, Ga., 144, 145

Sapelo Sound, Ga., 69, 70, 77, 84, 85, 97, 102, 105, 108, 110, 111, 122, 137, 140, 148
Savannah, CSS, 154
Savannah, Ga., 3, 4, 6–9, 12, 13, 83, 86, 89–91, 93, 97, 98, 101–3, 105, 110, 111, 147, 151, 152, 154–56, 165
Savannah Navy Yard, 152, 154
Semmes, Alexander A., 107, 108, 111, 120, 123, 128, 132, 135–37, 142, 149, 160
Sherman, Thomas W., 3
Sieniewicz, Harry, 158
South Hampton Plantation, 127, 138
South Newport, Ga., 66, 127, 132
South Newport River, Ga., 116
Spaulding Plantation, 106–7
Spencers Island, N.S., 25, 28
Standard (brigantine), 39–41, 43, 45, 47, 49, 51, 55, 57–60, 62, 64, 65, 67, 69, 70, 73, 74, 77–89, 93, 96, 97, 99, 100, 101, 103–5, 110, 112, 113, 117, 118, 124–26, 128–32, 142, 145, 150, 151, 154, 155, 162, 163, 165, 167
Stephens, William, 13, 15, 16, 18
Stevens, William C., 120
Sunbury, Ga., 66, 88, 151
Susquehanna, USS, 11

Tahoma, USS, 149
Thomson, William, 111, 150

Union, USS, 4, 5, 105

Waldburg, Jacob, 83, 86
Walthour, William L., 109, 111, 115, 124
Wamsutta, USS, 106, 108–11, 115, 120, 122–25, 127, 128, 132, 134–42, 149, 156

Warnell, James S., 116, 127–29, 133, 138

Watmough, Pendleton G., 98–100, 102, 105, 110, 111, 113, 114, 120–23, 128, 140, 142, 148, 149

Way, Edgar, 134

Weehawken, USS, 152, 153

Willie (schooner), 109

Windsor, N.S., 27, 30, 31, 33, 39

Winn, Abial, 111

Woodville Plantation, 114–16, 122, 136–38

Yonge, William H. H., 162

Zoucks, John E., 130